I N T E R W E A V E
P R E S E N T S

crocheted gifts

Irresistible Projects to Make & Give

INTERWEAVE

EDITOR
anne merrow

COVER & INTERIOR DESIGN
pamela norman

PHOTOGRAPHY
joe hancock

PHOTO STYLING
pamela chavez

WARDROBE STYLING/HAIR & MAKEUP
carol beaver

TECHNICAL EDITOR
julie holetz

ILLUSTRATIONS
gayle ford

STITCH DIAGRAMS
karen manthey

PRODUCTION DESIGN & LAYOUT
katherine jackson

Interweave Press LLC
201 East Fourth Street
Loveland, CO 80537-5655 USA
interweavestore.com

Printed in China by Asia Pacific Offset.

Library of Congress Cataloging-in-Publication Data

Werker, Kim P.
 Crocheted gifts : irresistible projects to
    make and give / Kim Werker.
      p. cm.
 Includes bibliographical references and index.
 ISBN 978-1-59668-107-1
 1. Crocheting. I. Title.
 TT825.W457 2009
 746.43'4--dc22
                         2009003455

10 9 8 7 6 5 4 3 2 1

dedication

To Grandma Shirley, to Olivia Madelyn, and to all the designers who make gifts so wonderful to give.

acknowledgments

I consider it a gift, indeed, to work with the designers featured in these pages. Their creativity and passion for crochet are the foundation of the craft, and I thank them for their contributions to this book.

Likewise, to work with Interweave is always a true pleasure. To my editor Anne Merrow and to Rebecca Campbell and Tricia Waddell, thank you!

kim werker

contents

the gift of giving

About a year before this book went to press, when I was in the thick of preparing the manuscript, my good friend had a baby early on a Tuesday morning. As if seized by an uncontrollable force, I closed my laptop and hunted down my trusted cone of baby-friendly yarn. I began crocheting. I had to. I had no choice; the mysterious force made me do it. Several hours later I had a lovely round lace blanket just big enough to wrap her tiny body. At least, it would be just big enough to wrap her tiny body for about three weeks before she would outgrow it. So I told myself—and wee Olivia's somewhat baffled but humoring parents—that she could use it as a travel blanket when she's a toddler, since it's small enough that it won't drag on the ground.

This book is full of projects for just such a special occasion and for the more mundane occasions we must conjure when we're compelled to crochet for the people we love. Some of the most talented crochet designers contributed their take on a most welcome gift, be it for a specific occasion like a wedding or housewarming, or just because. Ranging from one-skein whimsies in luxurious yarns to garments, you'll have many opportunities to keep your hands and mind happy while creating something to show how much you love someone. Whether an intricate project or a quick, last-minute one, no matter how far in advance you're planning, you'll find the perfect gift in these pages. ꙮ

mitts
FOR THE
WHOLE FAMILY

A gift of warmth is always satisfying for both giver and recipient. Nice, big shells made of nice, big, fluffy yarn form the comfortable cuff of these warm mittens. Sized for the whole family and quick to stitch, each pair requires only one skein of yarn. Let color do the work for you as you outfit everyone you know.

FINISHED SIZE Child's (women's, men's): 8 (10, 12)" [20 (25, 30) cm] from cuff to top of mitten; 7 (8, 9½)" [18 (20.5, 24) cm] circumference around widest part of hand.

YARN Worsted weight (Medium #4), about 110 (200, 215) yd (100 [183, 196.5] m).

Shown here: Malabrigo Worsted

(100% merino wool; 215 yd [195 m]/ 100 g): Frank Ochre #35 (yellow; A), Olive #56 (green; B), and Paris Night #52 (blue; C), 1 skein for each pair.

HOOK Size K/10.5 (6.5 mm). Adjust hook size if necessary to obtain the correct gauge.

NOTIONS Removable stitch marker (m); tapestry needle.

GAUGE 13 sts and 11 rows = 4" (10 cm) in hdc.

NOTE

+ Mittens are worked in joined rounds without turning.

stitch guide

+ SHELL (SH)
(3 dc, ch 1, 3 dc) in same st or sp.

+ CUFF STITCH PATTERN
(mult of 8 + 7 ch)
Rnd 1: Ch 3 (counts as first dc here and throughout), *sk next
3 ch, sh (see above) in next ch, sk 3 ch, dc in next ch; rep
from * around omitting final dc, sl st in beg ch-3 to join.
Rnd 2: Ch 3, sh in first ch-1 sp, *dc in next dc, sh in next ch-1 sp;
rep from * around, ending with sl st in beg ch-3.
Rep Rnd 2 for pattern.

MITTEN
Ch 24 (32, 40), sl st in first ch to form a ring.
Note: Place marker (pm) in top of beg ch to mark beg of
rnd; move m up as work progresses.

Cuff
Work cuff st patt (see Stitch Guide) for 4 (5, 6) rnds—3 (4,
5) sh.

Hand
Rnd 1: Ch 2 (counts as hdc here and throughout), hdc in
each dc of sh, sk each ch-1 sp and single dc, sl st in beg
ch-2 to join—19 (25, 31) hdc.
Rnd 2: Ch 2, hdc in each st around, sl st in beg ch-2 to join.
Rep Rnd 2 two (three, four) more times. Fasten off.

Thumb
Rnd 1: Ch 2 (2, 3), hdc in 1 (2, 2) hdc before m, hdc in
marked st, hdc in 1 (2, 2) hdc after m, ch 2 (2, 3), sl st
in first ch to join—3 (5, 5) hdc.
Rnd 2: Ch 2, hdc in each ch and hdc around—7 (9, 11) sts.
Work 2 (3, 4) more rounds even in hdc.

Shape thumb top
Ch 2, hdc2tog (see Glossary) 3 (4, 5) times around, sl st in
beg ch-2 to join—4 (5, 6) hdc.

Fasten off, leaving a 6" (15 cm) tail. With yarn needle and
tail, gather up rem sts and pull tight to close top of thumb.

Continue hand
With RS facing, join yarn with sl st in center ch at base of
thumb, ch 2, hdc in bottom ridge lp of first 2 (2, 3) ch of
thumb, hdc2tog over side of st joining hand and thumb and
next free stitch of hand, hdc around hand to last st before
thumb, hdc2tog over last st of hand and st joining hand
and thumb, hdc in bottom ridge lp of next 2 (2, 3) ch of
thumb, sl st in beg ch-2 to join—21 (25, 33) hdc.
Work 6 (8, 10) more rounds even in hdc.

Shape hand
Next rnd: Ch 2, hdc2tog 8 (12, 16) times—11 (13, 17) sts.
Work 1 rnd even in hdc.
Next rnd: Ch 2, hdc2tog 5 (6, 8) times—6 (7, 9) sts. Fasten
off, leaving 6" (15 cm) tail. With tail threaded on
tapestry needle, gather up rem sts and pull tight to
close top of hand.

FINISHING
Weave in loose ends, being sure to secure top of hand and
thumb. Gently steam block, if necessary, to smooth and
shape.

Cuff Stitch Pattern

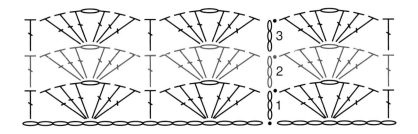

= chain (ch)

= slip stitch (sl st)

= double crochet (dc)

mesh
trellis
CARDIGAN

A garment can be a tricky gift to give. As the maker, you have it easy. You get to stitch lovingly and seam with care. But you might not want this gift to be a surprise, so you can be sure the recipient will love it. Check with her about the size and color she prefers. And don't forget that sometimes the greatest gift you can give is one to yourself.

FINISHED SIZE 36 (41, 45, 48, 56)" (91.5 [104, 114.5, 122, 142] cm) bust circumference; to fit sizes 32–34 (36–38, 40–42, 44–46, 48–50)" (81–86.5 [91.5–96.5, 101.5–106.5, 112–117, 122–127] cm).

YARN Worsted weight (Medium #4), about 900 (1,050, 1,100, 1,250, 1,300) yd (823 [960, 1,006, 1,143, 1,189] m).

Shown here: Red Heart Eco-Ways (70% acrylic, 30% recycled polyester; 186 yd [170 m]/4 oz): aquarium #3520, 5 (6, 6, 7, 7) skeins.

HOOK Size G/6 (4 mm) (H/8 [5 mm], H/8 [5 mm], H/8 [5 mm], I/9 [5.5 mm]) for size 36 (41, 45, 48, 56)" (91.5 [104, 114.5, 122, 142] cm), respectively.

NOTIONS Tapestry needle; sewing needle and matching thread; two ⅝" (1.5 cm) buttons.

GAUGE Size 36" (91.5 cm): 8 reps and 8 rows = 4" (10 cm) in dc mesh patt with smallest hook.

Sizes 41 (45, 48)" (104 [114.5, 122] cm): 7 reps and 7 rows = 4" (10 cm) in dc mesh patt with medium hook.

Size 56" (142 cm): 6 reps and 6 rows = 4" (10 cm) in dc mesh patt with largest hook.

NOTE
+ Use hook size as indicated for your size.

LOWER BODICE

Beg at under-bust and work down in fan trellis patt as foll:
With appropriate size hook (see Notes), ch 146 (146, 158, 170, 170).

Row 1: (WS) Sc in bottom ridge lp of 2nd ch from hook, *ch 5, sk 3 ch, sc in next ch; rep from * across, turn—36 (36, 39, 42, 42) ch-5 sps.

Row 2: Ch 5 (counts as dc, ch 2), sc in first ch-5 sp, *7 dc in next ch-5 sp, sc in next ch-5 sp**, ch 5, sc in next ch-5 sp; rep from * to last sc ending at **; ch 2, dc in last sc, turn.

Row 3: Ch 1, sc in first dc, *ch 5, skip next dc, sc in next dc, ch 5, skip 3 dc, sc in next dc, ch 5**, sc in next ch-5 sp; rep from * to last sp ending at **; sc in 3rd ch of tch, turn.

Rows 4–19: Rep Rows 2–3 eight more times.

Row 20: Rep Row 2. Fasten off.

UPPER BODICE

Work up from under-bust in dc mesh patt as foll:

Row 1: With RS facing and working in rem lps of foundation ch, join yarn in first ch, ch 4 (counts as dc, ch 1 here and throughout), dc in next ch-5 sp, ch 1, * [dc, ch 1] 2 times in next ch-5 sp; rep from * to last sp; dc in last sp, ch 1, dc in last ch, turn—72 (72, 78, 84, 84) dc.

Rows 2–4 (4, 4, 6, 6): Ch 4, *dc in next dc, ch 1; rep from * to last st, dc in 3rd ch of tch; turn.

Shape fronts and back

Row 1: (RS; dec row) Ch 4, dc2tog (see Glossary) over next 2 dc, *ch 1, dc in next dc; rep from * to last 3 dc; ch 1, dc2tog over next 2 dc, ch 1, dc in 3rd ch of tch; turn—70 (70, 76, 82, 82) dc.

Row 2: Ch 4, *dc in next dc, ch 1; rep from * to last st, dc in 3rd ch of tch; turn.

Divide for fronts and back as foll:

Right front

Row 3: (RS) Ch 4, dc2tog over next 2 dc, [ch 1, dc in next dc] 15 (15, 16, 18, 18) times, turn—17 (17, 18, 20, 20) dc.

Row 4: Ch 4, *dc in next dc, ch 1; rep from * to last st, dc in 3rd ch of tch; turn.

Row 5: Ch 4, dc2tog over next 2 dc, ch 1, * dc in next dc,

ch 1; rep from * to last st; dc in 3rd ch of tch; turn—16
(16, 17, 19, 19).

Rows 6–19 (19, 19, 21, 21): Rep Rows 4–5—9 (9, 10, 11, 11)
dc. Fasten off.

Back

Row 3: With RS facing, join yarn in next available dc of
Row 2 of front-slope shaping, ch 4, [dc in next dc, ch 1]
32 (32, 36, 38, 38) times, ch 1, dc in next dc, turn—34
(34, 38, 40, 40) dc.

Rows 4–19 (19, 19, 21, 21): Ch 4, *dc in next dc, ch 1; rep
from * to last st, dc in 3rd ch of tch, turn. Fasten off.

Left front

Row 3: With RS facing, join yarn in next available dc of
Row 2 of front-slope shaping, ch 4, *dc in next dc, ch 1;
rep from * to last 3 dc, dc2tog over next 2 dc, ch 1, dc
in 3rd ch of tch, turn—17 (17, 18, 20, 20) dc.

Row 4: Ch 4, *dc in next dc, ch 1; rep from * to last st, dc in
3rd ch of tch, turn.

Row 5: Ch 4, *dc in next dc, ch 1; rep from * to last 3
dc, dc2tog over next 2 dc, ch 1, dc in 3rd ch of tch,
turn—16 (16, 17, 19, 19) dc.

Rows 6–19 (19, 19, 21, 21): Rep Rows 4–5—9 (9, 10, 11, 11)
dc. Fasten off.

With RS tog and yarn threaded on a tapestry needle, sew
shoulder seams. Turn right side out.

SLEEVES

Sleeves are worked in turned rnds as foll:

Rnd 1: With RS facing, join yarn in top of dc to the left
of the front/back division, ch 4, *dc in next dc, ch 1;
rep from * around, sl st in 3rd ch of beg ch-4 to join,
turn—34 (34, 34, 38, 38) dc.

Rnd 2: Ch 4, *dc in next dc, ch 1; rep from * around, sl st in
3rd ch of beg ch-4 to join, turn.

Rnds 3–5 (5, 5, 7, 7): Rep Rnd 2.

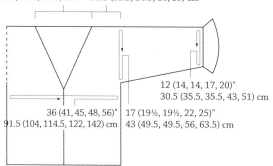

8 (9, 10, 10, 12)"
20.5 (23, 25.5, 25.5, 30.5) cm

4½ (5, 5¾, 6¼, 7½)"
11.5 (12.5, 14.5, 16, 19) cm

12 (14, 14, 17, 20)"
30.5 (35.5, 35.5, 43, 51) cm

36 (41, 45, 48, 56)"
91.5 (104, 114.5, 122, 142) cm

17 (19½, 19½, 22, 25)"
43 (49.5, 49.5, 56, 63.5) cm

Rnd 6 (6, 6, 8, 8): (dec rnd) Ch 4, dc2tog over next 2 dc, *ch 1, dc in next dc; rep from * to last 2 dc, ch 1, dc2tog, sl st in 3rd ch of beg ch-4 to join, turn—32 (32, 32, 36, 36) dc.

Work 5 rnds even in patt as established.

Next rnd: Rep dec rnd—30 (30, 30, 34, 34) dc.

Work 3 (3, 3, 5, 5) rnds even in patt as established.

Next rnd: Rep dec rnd—28 (28, 28, 32, 32) dc.

Work 3 (3, 3, 5, 5) rnds even in patt as established.

Next rnd: Rep dec rnd—26 (26, 26, 30, 30) dc.

Sizes 36 (41, 45)" (91.5 [104, 114.5] cm) only

Work 3 rnds even in patt as established.

Next rnd: Rep dec rnd—24 (24, 24) dc.

All sizes

Work 2 rnds even in est patt. Do not fasten off. Work fan trellis sleeve edging as foll:

Rnd 1: (RS) (Sl st, ch 1, sc) in first ch-1 sp, *ch 5, sc in next ch-1 sp, 7 dc in next ch-1 sp**, sc in next ch-1 sp; rep from * around ending at **, sl st in first sc to join, turn.

Rnd 2: Sl st in first dc, (sl st, ch 1, sc) in next dc, *ch 5, sk 3 dc, sc in next dc, ch 5, sc in next ch-5 sp, ch 5, sk next dc**, sc in next dc; rep from * around ending at **, sl st in first sc to join, turn.

Rnd 3: (Sl st, ch 1, sc) in first ch-5 sp, *ch 5, sc in next ch-5 sp, 7 dc in next ch-5 sp**, sc in next ch-5 sp; rep from * around ending at **, sl st in first sc to join, turn.

Rnds 4–5: Rep Rnds 2–3 but do not turn at the end of Rnd 5.

Rnd 6: Ch 1, working from left to right for reverse sc (rsc; see Glossary), rsc in each st and 3 rsc in each ch-5 sp around, sl st in first rsc to join. Fasten off.

FINISHING

Weave in loose ends.

Edging

Row 1: With RS facing, join yarn at corner of lower-right front, ch 1, sc evenly up the front, around the neck and down the left front to the corner, turn.

Row 2: Ch 1, sc in each sc to end of lower-right front, turn. Work rsc across bottom edge same as for Rnd 6 of sleeves to corner of left front, then up left front, around neck and down right front, increasing as needed at corners to keep work flat. Fasten off. Weave in loose ends.

Button loops

With RS facing, join yarn at first row of dc mesh sts in the rsc rnd on the right front; ch 6 or make a chain to accommodate buttons of choice, sl st in next rsc. Fasten off. Weave in loose ends.

Rep button lp at the 4th row of dc mesh sts.

With sewing needle and thread and using button loops as a guide, sew buttons on left front edging.

shawlette
IN CHAINS

*I*nspired by the delicate nature of a yarn so fine, this shawl uses a small hook but keeps the stitching simple so it's fun and quick to stitch. So often we gloss over the chain stitch and use it only as a means to get to another stitch. Worked in skinny columns joined with horizontal bands of long chains, this design is an homage to the chain stitch and results in a lovely and versatile accessory.

FINISHED SIZE 67" (170 cm) wide and 17" (43 cm) long from point to neck.

YARN Laceweight (Lace #0), about 800 yd (731.5 m).

Shown here: Jade Sapphire Lacey Lamb (100% lambswool; 825 yds [754 m]/60 g); golden-tan 109, 1 skein.

HOOK Size C/2 (2.75mm). Adjust hook size if necessary to obtain the correct gauge.

NOTIONS Stitch markers (m); tapestry needle.

GAUGE 24 ch and 5 rows = 3" (7.5 cm).

NOTES

+ The shawl is constructed of strips of double-treble stitches that are joined together with long chains throughout. The strips vary in length to form a triangle with short lengths at the edges and the longest lengths in the center.

+ Each row of a strip is only 4 dtr wide.

+ As you create the dtr strips, you are working from the bottom of the shawl to the top. However, when you join strips together, begin at the top of the shawl and work toward the bottom in order to form the triangular point at the center-bottom and the straight edge at the neck. To keep track of the top edge, mark the last row of each strip with a stitch marker (m).

+ When joining strips that differ in length, start with your hook in the end of the shorter strip. If you do not end the last row on the shorter side, simply adjust by omitting the last joining chain of the previous row or work one more.

stitch guide

+ DOUBLE TREBLE (DTR)
Yo 3 times, insert hook in indicated st or sp and pull up lp, [yo and draw through 2 lps] 3 times.

+ STRIP PATTERN
Row 1: Ch 5 (counts as first dtr here and throughout), 3 dtr in 5th ch from hook, turn—4 dtr.
Row 2: Sk 2 sts, sl st in sp between 2nd and 3rd dtr, ch 5, 3 dtr in same sp, turn—4 dtr.
Rep Row 2 for patt.

SHAWLETTE
Make Strips
Strip A (make 8)
Work strip patt (see Stitch Guide) for 6 rows. Fasten off.

Strip B (make 6)
Work strip patt for 12 rows. Fasten off.

Strip C (make 4)
Work strip patt for 18 rows. Fasten off.

Strip D (make 2)
Work strip patt for 24 rows. Fasten off.

Join strips
Following diagram on page 22, join strips using the appropriate joining method based on the length of the strip as foll:

Joining strips of equal length
Beg at the top (neck) edge of the shawl (see Notes). Join first strip to 2nd strip as foll: join yarn with sl st in edge of dtr at end of Row 1 of first strip, [ch 24, sl st in edge of dtr on Row 1 of second strip, ch 24, sl st in same sp of first strip] 3 times (you should have 6 ch linking the 2 strips tog), *[ch 24, sl st in edge of dtr on Row 2 of second strip, ch 24, sl st in edge of dtr on Row 2 of first strip] 3 times, rep from * for each row of the strips. Fasten off. Rep to join subsequent strips to previously joined strips of equal length.

Joining strips of unequal length

Rep as for joining strips of equal length until all rows of shorter strip are joined. Do not fasten off.

To blend the longer strip to a shorter strip, make sure you begin at the shorter strip, *ch 27, sl st in next row of longer strip, ch 27, sl st in same (last) row on shorter strip; rep from * increasing length of joining chain by 3 ch every time you go up to the next row until all rows of the longer strip have been worked. Fasten off.

FINISHING

Weave in loose ends. Block as desired.

Shawlette Assembly

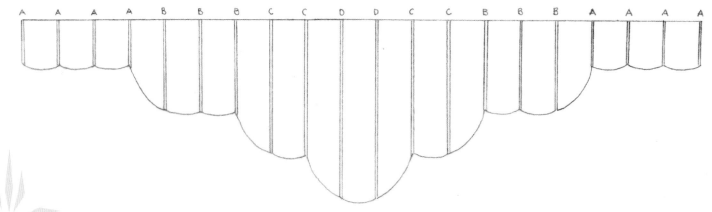

DESIGNER *katie himmelberg*

SEA STAR PENDANT

A classic flower motif set onto a crochet-covered ring is a quick gift for anyone who enjoys adorning herself with a bold necklace. Play with color and cord to create an infinite array of styles.

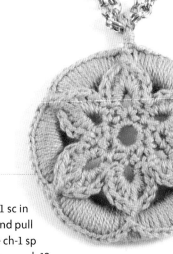

PENDANT
Motif

LP yarn tail behind working yarn to form an adjustable ring, yo and pull up.

Rnd 1 Ch 1, 12 sc in ring, sl st in first sc to join—12 sc.

Rnd 2 Ch 1, (sc, ch 5, sc, ch 1) in same stitch, *sk 1 sc, (sc, ch 5, sc, ch 1) in next sc as join; rep from * 4 more times, sl st in first sc to join—6 ch-sps.

Rnd 3 Ch 1, (sc, hdc, 4 dc, ch 2, 4 dc, hdc, sc) in each ch-5 sp around; sl st in first sc to join. Fasten off.

Ring

Beg with slipknot on hook, work 1 sc in plastic ring. *Insert hook in ring and pull up loop, insert hook through one ch-1 sp on point of motif, then complete sc, work 12 sc in ring. Rep from * 5 more times, sl st in first st to join, then ch 4 to create lp around metal chain, sl st in first sc to join. Fasten off, leaving a 10" (25.5 cm) tail. Wrap tail several times around lp below chain and weave in ends.

FINISHED SIZE 2" (5 cm) diameter.

YARN Fingering weight (Super Fine #1), about 35 yd (32 m).

Shown here: Karabella Lace Merino Silk (70% extrafine merino wool, 30% silk; 250 yd [230 m]/50 g): green #7185, 1 ball.

HOOK Size B/1(2.25 mm).

NOTIONS 2" (5 cm) diameter plastic ring; 60" (1.5 m) metal chain or other cord or necklace; tapestry needle.

wire hairpin-lace
BOWL

*W*ire lends strength and sturdiness to otherwise delicate hairpin lace in a bowl that's perfect as a housewarming or hostess gift. One side of a strip of hairpin lace is attached to a simple circle base. The other side is topped with a few rounds of single crochet.

FINISHED SIZE 3" (7.5 cm) bowl base diameter; 5½" (14 cm) bowl rim diameter; 2½" (6.5 cm) bowl height.

WIRE About 50 yd of 24-gauge copper wire or colored copper wire.

Shown here: 24-gauge craft wire (25 yd [23 m]): 2 spools.

HOOK Size 00 (3.50mm) steel hook.

NOTIONS Wire cutters; 2" (5 cm) hairpin lace loom; stitch marker (m).

GAUGE Bowl base diameter = 3" (7.5 cm).

Hairpin lace strip = 2" (5 cm) wide and 14" (35.5 cm) long, before assembly.

NOTES

+ Working with wire can be hard on your hands and your tools; take frequent breaks and be sure to use a hook you don't mind scratching.

+ Be sure that hairpin lace loops are not twisted when inserting hook to make rim or to join hairpin lace strip to base.

+ Weave in ends by using the wire itself as a needle to stitch back and forth a few times through adjacent stitches.

+ You may find it useful to protect your most-used fingers with an adhesive bandage, baby/dog finger toothbrush (with bristles turned out of the way), or specialty finger protector.

+ The bowl pictured was made with craft wire, but copper wire may be used. Copper wire is softer and easier to work with than craft wire. When made with copper wire, the bowl will be slightly less firm but will still hold its shape.

+ A U.S. size 00 (3.50mm) steel hook is the same size as a U.S. size E/4 (3.50mm) aluminum hook, but steel is much stronger and thus better for working with wire.

BOWL
Sidewall

Adjust hairpin lace loom to 2" (5 cm) wide and, leaving a 6" (15 cm) to 8" (20.5 cm) tail at both beginning and end, work a strip of hairpin lace (see sidebar on pages 27–29) with 64 loops on each side.

Form a ring with the hairpin lace strip by weaving in the tails to connect the ends. Cut the remainder of the tails close to work.

Base

Note: Do not join rounds of base. To keep your place, use a stitch marker in the first stitch of the round, moving the marker up as your work progresses.

Rnd 1: Form an adjustable ring by placing the tail end of the wire behind the working end to make a large ring, draw wire through ring, ch 1, 8 sc in ring, pull tail end to tighten ring.

Rnd 2: 2 sc in front lp only (flo) of each sc around—16 sc.

Rnd 3: *2 sc flo in next sc, sc flo in next sc; rep from * around—24 sc.

Rnd 4: *2 sc flo in next sc, sc flo in each of next 2 sc; rep from * around—32 sc.

Rnd 5: *2 sc flo in next sc, sc flo in each of next 3 sc; rep from * around—40 sc.

Rnd 6: *2 sc flo in next sc, sc flo in each of next 4 sc; rep from * around—48 sc. Do not fasten off. Remove hook from last loop, stretch and pull the base into an even and nicely shaped circle, and return hook to last loop. *Insert hook in (back lp only [blo] of next sc and 2 lps of hairpin lace), yo and draw through all lps on hook (this makes a sl st join), [insert hook in (blo of next sc and next lp of hairpin lace), yo and draw through all lps on hook] twice; rep from * around—48 sl sts. Fasten off and weave in loose ends.

Stretch and pull the piece to shape it so the base is flat and the sides begin to form a bowl-like shape.

Rim

Rnd 1: With outside of bowl facing you, insert hook in 1 lp of hairpin lace and pull up a lp, ch 1, 2 sc in same hairpin lp, *sc in each of next 7 hairpin lps, 2 sc in next hairpin lp; rep from * around ending with sc in each of last 7 hairpin lps, sl st in first sc to join, turn—72 sc.

Rnd 2: Ch 1, sc in each sc around, sl st in first sc to join, turn.

Rnds 3–4: Rep Rnd 2.

Fasten off and weave in loose ends.

FINISHING

Stretch and pull the bowl into shape.

HAIRPIN LACE

There is more than one method of making hairpin lace. Although the methods are quite similar, the resulting appearance of the hairpin lace strip is different, which is more conspicuous when working with wire due to its stiffness. Even if you're familiar with the technique, follow the instructions here to achieve the look of the bowl.

Working with Wire

When making hairpin lace with yarn, you turn the hook upside down in the center of the loom, flip the loom, and then turn the hook right side up again. When working with wire, its stiffness allows you to use a slightly easier method (see pages 28–29).

The nature of wire makes it easy to work too tightly on a hairpin lace loom, causing the loom to bow in the middle and resulting in a hairpin lace strip that is uneven in width. Working close to the top brace can help prevent this problem.

Set Up Loom

Hairpin lace looms have two prongs (left and right) and usually two braces (top and bottom). Insert the prongs into one of the braces at the indicated width. Make a slip knot, leaving the loop open half the width of the loom, and slide it over the left prong of the loom so the working end of the wire is in front of the right prong. Insert the prongs into the other brace.

Begin Hairpin Lace

Wrap the wire around the right prong from the front to the back of the loom, insert crochet hook into the left loop **(Figure 1)**, yarn over and draw up a loop, ch 1 **(Figure 2)**.

Remove hook from loop, place hook behind right prong, and reinsert hook in same loop. Keeping the hook in place, flip loom over from right to left (counterclockwise) **(Figure 3)** allowing wire to wrap around the right prong from front to back. Insert hook into left loop **(Figure 4)**, sc.

*Remove hook from loop, place hook behind right prong, and reinsert hook in same loop. Keeping hook in place, flip loom over from right to left (counterclockwise). Insert hook under entire left loop **(Figure 5)**, sc. Repeat from * until you have completed the indicated number of loops on both sides of the hairpin lace strip.

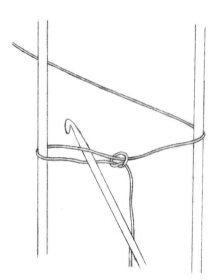

Figure 1

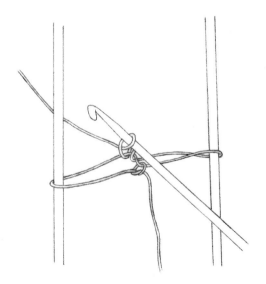

Figure 2

When the working space on the loom fills up, remove the brace from the bottom end of the loom and slide most of the loops off, leaving at least two loops on each side of the loom, replace the brace, and continue working.

Finishing

When hairpin lace strip is complete, fasten off and remove all loops from loom.

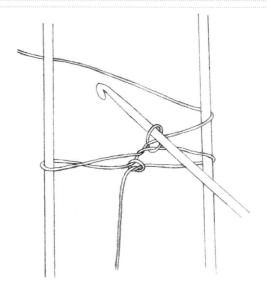

Figure 3

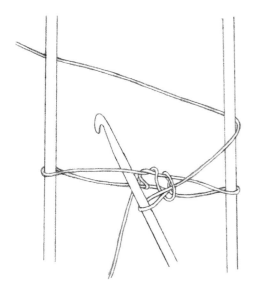

Figure 4

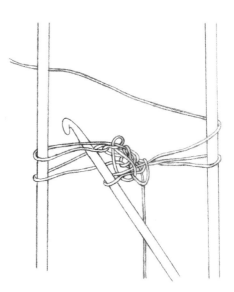

Figure 5

berry baby

HAT AND BOOTIES

$\mathcal{A}$dorable babywear hardly needs to be precious. This hat-and-booties pair are gender-neutral and sure to be well-worn and well-loved. The booties are perfect for first-time footwear makers; they're worked toe-up and the heel shaping is deceptively simple. The hat is topped with leaves to match those in the booties, and it's sized to fit even adults who enjoy embracing their inner whimsy.

FINISHED SIZE *Booties:* 3¼ (4¼)" (8.5 [11] cm) long, to fit foot up to 3 (4)" (7.5 [10] cm). For ages newborn (1–3 months).

Hat: 12 (14, 16, 19, 21, 23)" (30.5 [35.5, 40.5, 53.5, 58.5] cm) circumference at brim. For ages preemie (newborn, 0–3 months, 3–9 months, 9+ months/small child, larger child/ adult).

YARN DK weight (Light #3), about 14 yd [13 m] in main color and 7 yd [6 m] in contrast color for booties; about 60 (85, 100, 136, 172, 204) yd (55 [78, 90, 125, 157, 187] m] in main color and 20 (60, 60, 60, 60, 60) yd (18 [55, 55, 55, 55] m] for hat.

Shown here: Rowan Pure Wool DK (100% wool, 136 yd [125 m]/50 g): pomegranate 029 (red), less than 1 skein for booties and 1 (1, 1, 1, 2, 2) for hat, and glade 021 (green), less than 1 skein for booties and 1 skein for hat.

HOOK Size F/5 (3.75mm). Adjust hook size if necessary to obtain the correct gauge.

NOTIONS Stitch marker (m); tapestry needle.

GAUGE 18 sts and 22 rounds = 4" (10 cm) in sc.

NOTES

+ Beg ch does not count as a st throughout patt.

+ Booties, hat, and foliage are crocheted in a spiral without joining rnds. To help keep track of rounds, place a stitch marker (m) in the first st of the rnd to mark the beg of the rnd. Move m up as work progresses.

BOOTIES

With red, ch 2.

Rnd 1: 5 sc in 2nd ch from hook, place marker (pm; see Notes) in first st, do not join—5 sts.

Rnd 2: 2 sc in each st around—10 sts.

Rnd 3: 2 sc in each st around—20 sts.

Rnds 4–10 (4–14): Sc in each st around.

Rnd 11 (15): Sc in each st around, turn.

Shape opening

Row 1: Ch 1, sc in next 15 sts, turn leaving rem sts unworked—15 sts.

Rows 2–6: Ch 1, sc in each st across, turn—15 sts.

Shape heel

Row 1: Ch 1, sc in next 5 sts, sc2tog (see Glossary) over next 2 sts, sc in next st, sc2tog over next 2 sts, sc to end, turn—13 sts rem.

Row 2: Ch 1, sc in next 4 sts, sc2tog over next 2 sts, sc in next st, sc2tog over next 2 sts, sc to end, turn—11 sts rem.

Row 3: Ch 1, sc in next 4 sts, sc3tog (see Glossary) over next 3 sts (see Glossary), sc to end, turn—9 sts rem.

Fasten off, leaving a tail several inches long. Bring edges of last row together and, with tail threaded on a tapestry needle, use whipstitch (see Glossary) to sew back seam (see drawing opposite).

Leaf and Top of Bootie

Beg leaf: With green, ch 2.

Row 1: 2 sc in second ch from hook, turn—2 sts.

Row 2: Ch 1, 2 sc in each st across, turn—4 sts.

Row 3: Ch 1, 2 sc in first st, sc in next 2 sts, 2 sc in next st, turn—6 sts.

Rows 4–6: Ch 1, sc in each st across, turn.

Row 7: Ch 1, sc2tog over first 2 sts, sc in next 2 sts, sc2tog over next 2 sts, turn—4 sts rem.

Row 8: Ch 1, sc2tog over first 2 sts, sc2tog over next 2 sts, turn—2 sts rem.

Row 9: Ch 1, sc2tog over rem 2 sts, turn—1 st rem.

Leaf edging

With yarn still attached, ch 1, work sc edging around leaf as foll: sc in end of each row, (sc, ch 1, sc) in tip of leaf, ch 1, do not fasten off—20 sc.

Bootie edging

With RS of bootie facing, join yarn and leaf with sl st to front right corner of bootie for one bootie and front left corner of bootie for the other. Ch 1, work 25 sc evenly around opening of bootie, working 1 sc in end of each row and in each of the 5 unworked sts from the toe-up section of the bootie, sl st in first sc to join.

Rnd 1: Ch 1 (counts as first hdc), hdc in each st around, sl st in beg ch-1 to join—25 sts.

Rnd 2: Ch 2 (counts as first dc), dc in each st around, sl st in top of beg ch-2 to join.

Fasten off and weave in loose ends.

HAT

With red, ch 2.

Rnd 1: 5 sc in 2nd ch from hook, place marker (pm; see Notes) in first st, do not join—5 sc.

Rnd 2: 2 sc in each st around—10 sc.

Rnd 3: 2 sc in each st around—20 sc.

Rnd 4: Sc in each st around.

Rnd 5: 2 sc in each st around—40 sc.

Rnds 6–7: Sc in each st around.

Preemie size only

Rnd 8: *2 sc in next st, sc in next 3 sts; rep from * around—50 sts.

Rnds 9–13: Sc in each st around.

Rnd 14: *2 sc in next st, sc in next 9 sts; rep from * around—55 sts.

Rnd 15: Sc in each st around.

Rep Rnd 15 ten more times or to desired length, sl st in next st. Fasten off.

Preemie-size hat

0–3 month-size hat

Rep Rnd 16 fourteen more times or to desired length, sl st in next st. Fasten off.

3–9 month size only
Rnd 8: *2 sc in next st, sc in next st; rep from * around—60 sts.
Rnds 9–13: Sc in each st around.
Rnd 14: *2 sc in next st, sc in next 2 sts; rep from * around—80 sts.
Rnd 15–20: Sc in each st around.
Rnd 21: *2 sc in next st, sc in next 15 sts; rep from * around—85 sts.
Rnd 22: Sc in each st around.
Rep Rnd 22 twelve more times or to desired length, sl st in next st. Fasten off.

9+ month/child size only
Rnd 8: *2 sc in next st, sc in next st; rep from * around—60 sts.
Rnds 9–13: Sc in each st around.
Rnd 14: *2 sc in next st, sc in next st; rep from * around—90 sts.
Rnds 15–20: Sc in each st around.
Rnd 21: *2 sc in next st, sc in next 17 sts; rep from * around—95 sts.
Rnd 22: Sc in each st around.
Rep Rnd 22 sixteen more times or to desired length, sl st in next st. Fasten off.

Older child/adult size only
Rnd 8: *2 sc in next st, sc in next st; rep from * around—60 sts.
Rnds 9–13: Sc in each st around.
Rnd 14: *2 sc in next st, sc in next st; rep from * around—90 sts.
Rnds 15–20: Sc in each st around.
Rnd 21: *2 sc in next st, sc in next 5 sts; rep from * around—105 sts.
Rnd 22: Sc in each st around.
Rep Rnd 22 twenty more times or to desired length, sl st in next st. Fasten off.

Newborn size only
Rnd 8: *2 sc in next st, sc in next st; rep from * around—60 sts.
Rnds 9–14: Sc in each st around.
Rnd 15: *2 sc in next st, sc in next 11 sts; rep from * around—65 sts.
Rnd 16: Sc in each st around.
Rep Rnd 16 twelve more times or to desired length, sl st in next st. Fasten off.

0–3 month size only
Rnd 8: *2 sc in next st, sc in next st; rep from * around—60 sts.
Rnds 9–14: Sc in each st around.
Rnd 15: *2 sc in next st, sc in next 3 sts; rep from * around—75 sts.
Rnd 16: Sc in each st around.

Leaves
Preemie size only
With green, ch 2.

Rnd 1: 5 sc in 2nd ch from hook, pm in first st, do not join—5 sc.

Rnds 2–6: Sc in each st around.

Rnd 7: 2 sc in each st around—10 sc.

Rnd 8: 2 sc in each st around, turn—20 sc.

Work leaf section back and forth in rows.

Row 1: Ch 1, sc in next 3 sts, turn leaving rem sts unworked—3 sc.

Row 2: Ch 1, 2 sc in first st, sc in next st, 2 sc in next st, turn—5 sc.

Row 3: Ch 1, 2 sc in first st, sc in next 3 sts, 2 sc in next st, turn—7 sc.

Row 4–6: Ch 1, sc in each st across, turn.

Row 7: Ch 1, sc2tog (see Glossary) over first 2 sts, sc in next 3 sts, sc2tog over next 2 sts, turn—5 sts rem.

Row 8: Ch 1, sc2tog over first 2 sts, sc in next st, sc2tog over next 2 sts, turn—3 sts rem.

Row 9: Ch 1, sc2tog over first 2 sts, sc in next st, turn—2 sts rem.

Row 10: Ch 1, sc2tog over rem 2 sts, turn—1 st.

Work leaf edging as foll: Without fastening off, ch 1 and work sc edging around the leaf toward the stem, around the stem, and back up to the tip of the leaf as foll: sc in end of each leaf-row, sc in each st around stem as desired. Fasten off.

All other sizes
With green, ch 2.

Rnd 1: 5 sc in 2nd ch from hook, pm in first st, do not join—5 sts.

Rnd 2: Sc in each st around.

Rnd 3: 2 sc in each st around—10 sts.

Rnds 4–9: Sc in each st around.

Rnd 10: 2 sc in each st around—20 sts.

Rnd 11: Sc in each st around, turn.

Work leaf section back and forth in rows.

Row 1: Ch 1, sc in next 3 sts, turn leaving rem sts un-worked—3 sts.

Row 2: Ch 1, 2 sc in first st, sc in next st, 2 sc in next st, turn—5 sts.

Row 3: Ch 1, 2 sc in first st, sc in next 3 sts, 2 sc in next st, turn—7 sts.

Row 4: Ch 1, sc in each st across, turn.

Row 5: Ch 1, 2 sc in first st, sc in next 5 sts, 2 sc in next st, turn—9 sts.

Row 6–8: Ch 1, sc in each st across, turn.

Row 9: Ch 1, sc2tog (see Glossary) over first 2 sts, sc in next 5 sts, sc2tog over next 2 sts, turn—7 sts rem.

Row 10: Ch 1, sc in each st across, turn.

Row 11: Ch 1, sc2tog over first 2 sts, sc in next 3 sts, sc2tog over next 2 sts, turn—5 sts rem.

Row 12: Ch 1, sc2tog over first 2 sts, sc in next st, sc2tog over next 2 sts, turn—3 sts rem.

Row 13: Ch 1, sc2tog over first 2 sts, sc in next st, turn—2 sts rem.

Row 14: Ch 1, sc2tog over rem 2 sts, ch 1—1 st rem. Fasten off.

*With WS facing, join green in 2nd st of stem from last leaf worked, sc in same st and in each of next 2 sts, rep Rows 2–12, fasten off; rep from * for 3 more leaves but do not fasten off final leaf.

Work leaf edging as foll: Beg on final leaf, ch 1 and work sc edging around leaves and stem as foll: sc in end of each leaf-row, (sc, ch 1, sc) in tip of each leaf, sc in each st around stem as desired. Fasten off.

FINISHING
Booties
Block leaves by wetting and pinning flat to dry or by carefully ironing flat.

If the booties tend to slip off the baby's wiggly feet, you may wish to weave a length of the yarn in and out between the dc or hdc posts and tie it in a bow at the front of the booties.

Hat
Weave in loose ends. Block leaves flat.

With green yarn threaded on a tapestry needle, sew leaves to top of hat, weave in loose ends.

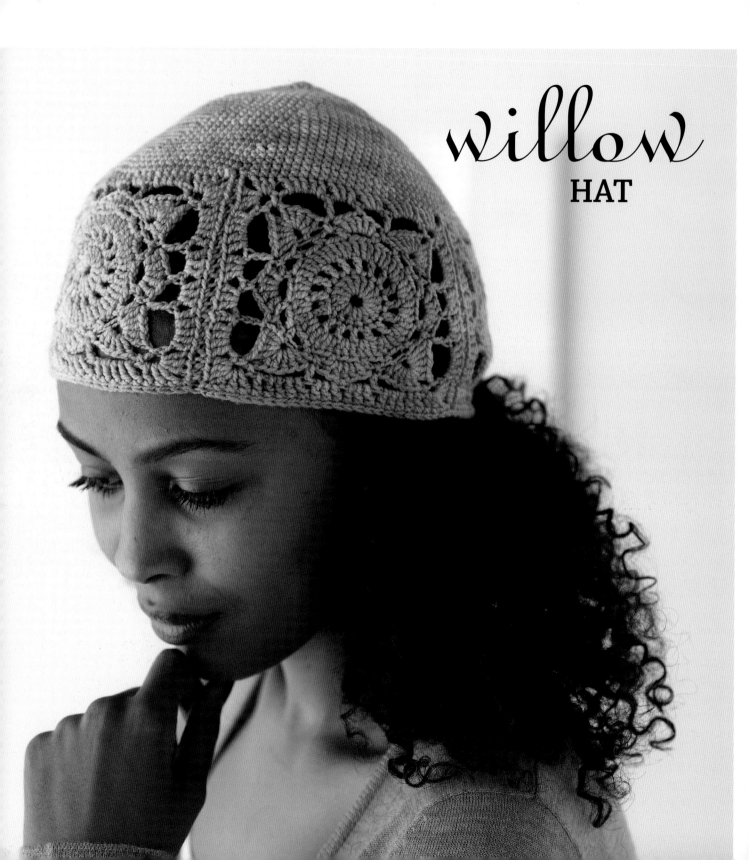

willow
HAT

*T*he feminine motifs at the brim of this hat frame the face beautifully. A simple single crochet crown finishes the cap off nicely, and the edging is a simple execution of single crochet and slip stitch. Designed for fingering-weight yarn, this little accessory is a gift sure to be loved.

FINISHED SIZE 16 (20, 24)" (40.5 [51, 61] cm) circumference at brim.

YARN Fingering weight (Super Fine #1), about 190 (275, 350) yd (174 [251, 320] m).

Shown here: Shibui Sock (100% Superwash Merino, 191 yd [175 m]/ 50 g): sky #3115, 1 (2, 2) skeins.

HOOK Size D/3 (3.25 mm). Adjust hook size if necessary to obtain correct gauge.

NOTIONS Tapestry needle; removable stitch marker (m).

GAUGE Willow square (see Stitch Guide) = 4" (10 cm) square.

NOTE

+ The crown is worked in a spiral without joining rounds and may be a bit pointy until blocked. Block hat on a head form or your own head to smooth the point.

stitch guide

+ **WILLOW SQUARE**—Ch 6, sl st in first ch to form ring.

Rnd 1: Ch 3 (counts as dc here and throughout), 15 dc in ring, sl st in 3rd ch of beg ch-3 to join—16 dc.

Rnd 2: Ch 4 (counts as dc, ch 1), [dc in next dc, ch 1] 15 times, sl st in 3rd ch of beg ch-4 to join—16 ch-1 sps.

Rnd 3: Ch 3, [2 dc in next ch-1 sp, dc in next dc] 15 times, 2 dc in last ch-1 sp, sl st in 3rd ch of beg ch-3 to join—48 dc.

Rnd 4: Ch 1, sc in same ch as join, *ch 5, sl st in 5th ch from hook, sk 2 dc, sc in next dc, ch 2, sk next 2 dc, sc in next dc, ch 3, sk next 2 dc, sc in next dc, ch 2, sk next 2 dc, **sc in next dc; rep from * 2 times then from * to ** once, sl st in first sc to join.

Rnd 5: Sl st in next ch-5 sp, ch 3, [4 dc, ch 3, 5 dc] in same sp, *sc in next ch-2 sp, 5 dc in next ch-3 sp, sc in next ch-2 sp, **[5 dc, ch 3, 5 dc] in next ch-5 sp; rep from * 2 times then from * to ** once, sl st in 3rd ch of beg ch-3 to join.

Rnd 6: Ch 3, *ch 5, [sc, ch 3, sc] in next ch-3 sp, ch 5, dc in next sc, ch 3, sk next 2 dc, sc in next dc, sk next 2 dc, ch 3**, dc in next sc; rep from * 2 times then from * to ** once, sl st in 3rd ch of beg ch-3 to join.

Rnd 7: Sl st in next ch-5 sp, ch 3, 4 dc in same sp, *[3 dc, ch 2, 3 dc] in next ch-3 sp, 5 dc in next ch-5 sp, 3 dc in each of next 2 ch-3 sps**, 5 dc in next ch-5 sp; rep from * 2 times then from * to ** once, sl st in 3rd ch of beg ch-3 to join. Fasten off.

Rnd 2 and all even rnds: Sc in each sc around.

Rnd 3: *Sc in next 9 (12, 15) sc, sc2tog; rep from * around—80 (104, 128) sts rem.

Rnd 5 *Sc in next 8 (11, 14) sc, sc2tog; rep from * around—72 (96, 120) sts rem.

Rnd 7: *Sc in next 7 (10, 13) sc, sc2tog; rep from * around—64 (88, 112) sts rem.

Rnd 9: *Sc in next 6 (9, 12) sc, sc2tog; rep from * around—56 (80, 104) sts rem.

Rnd 11: *Sc in next 5 (8, 11) sc, sc2tog; rep from * around—48 (72, 96) sts rem.

Rnd 13: *Sc in next 4 (7, 10) sc, sc2tog; rep from * around—40 (64, 88) sts rem.

Rnd 15: *Sc in next 3 (6, 9) sc, sc2tog; rep from * around—32 (56, 80) sts rem.

Rnd 17: *Sc in next 2 (5, 8) sc, sc2tog; rep from * around—24 (48, 72) sts rem.

Rnd 19: *Sc in next 1 (4, 7) sc, sc2tog; rep from * around—16 (40, 64) sts rem.

Rnd 21: *Sc in next 0 (3, 6) sc, sc2tog; rep from * around—8 (32, 56) sts rem.

HAT

Make 4 (5, 6) willow squares (see Stitch Guide). Sew squares into a band as foll: With RS of 2 squares tog, whipstitch (see Glossary) back lps of corresponding first and last ch sts and edge dc sts of one side of each square. Rep until all squares are joined; join the first square to the last to close the band. Join yarn at edge of one square and work 96 (120, 144) sc around edge of band working 1 sc in each dc and 1 sc in each corner ch sp. Do not join, place marker (pm) in last st to mark end of rnd; move m up as work progresses. Work 1 rnd of sc.

Shape crown

Rnd 1: *Sc in next 10 (13, 16) sc, sc2tog (see Glossary); rep from * around—88 (112, 136) sts rem.

Size 16" (40.5 cm) only
Fasten off, leaving a long tail.

Sizes 20 (24)" (51 [61] cm) only
Rnd 23: *Sc in next 2 (5) sc, sc2tog; rep from * around—24 (48) sts rem.

Rnd 25: *Sc in next 1 (4) sc, sc2tog; rep from * around—16 (40) sts rem.

Rnd 27: *Sc in next 0 (3) sc, sc2tog; rep from * around—8 (32) sts rem.

Size 20" (51 cm) only
Fasten off, leaving a long tail.

Size 24" (61 cm) only
Rnd 29: *Sc in next 2 sc, sc2tog; rep from * around—24 sts rem.

Rnd 31: *Sc, sc2tog; rep from * around—16 sts rem.

Rnd 33: Sc2tog around—8 sts rem. Fasten off, leaving a long tail.

All sizes
With tail threaded on a tapestry needle, draw tail through rem sts and pull tight to close. Weave in loose ends.

FINISHING
Join yarn in any st of motif brim, sc in each sc and corner ch of brim, as in first rnd of crown—96 (120, 144) sc.

Last rnd: Sl st in each sc around. Fasten off. Weave in loose ends. Block (see Notes).

Willow Square

⟳ = chain (ch)

• = slip stitch (sl st)

X = single crochet (sc)

┬ = double crochet (dc)

ORGANIC INDULGENCE WASHCLOTHS

These luscious washcloths are as satisfying to make as they are to give. Explore texture and color using luxurious and eco-friendly organic cotton while making perfect little gifts.

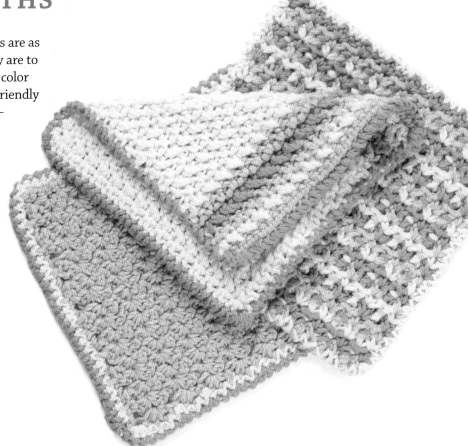

FINISHED SIZE About 10" (25.5 cm) square.

YARN Worsted (Medium #4), about 110 yd (101 m) for each washcloth. *Shown here:* Blue Sky Alpacas Organic Cotton (100% cotton; 150 yd [137 m]/ 100 g): bone #80 (A); sand #81 (B); nut #82 (C), 1 skein each.

HOOK Size I/9 (5.5 mm). Adjust hook size if necessary to obtain correct gauge.

GAUGE Striped: 14 sts and 9½ rows = 4" (10 cm) in patt. Solid: 3½ sts and 8 rows = 4" (10 cm) in trp-sh (see Stitch Guide). Tricolor: 8 sts and 10 rows = 4" (10 cm) in patt.

STITCH GUIDE

+ SHELL (SH)
(Sc, ch 2, sc) in same st.

+ FRONT POST DC (FPDC)
Yo, insert hook from front to back to front around post of next st, yo and pull up lp, [yo and draw through 2 lps] 2 times.

+ TRIPLE SHELL (TRP-SH)
(Sc, [ch 2, sc] 3 times) in same st.

STRIPED WASHCLOTH

With B, ch 33 (or mult of 2 sts + 1).

Row 1: Working in bottom ridge lps of ch, sc in 2nd ch from hook and in each ch across, change to A, turn—32 sc.

Row 2: Ch 1, hdc in first st, *sk next sc, dc in next st, working behind dc just made, sc in skipped sc; rep from * to last st, hdc in last st, turn—15 dc and sc, 2 hdc.

Rep Row 2 until piece measures 9½" (24 cm), using colors B, C, B for next 3 rows, then A to end. At end, change to C. Cont with Edging.

SOLID WASHCLOTH

With B, ch 37 (or mult of 4 sts + 1).

Row 1: Working in bottom ridge lps of ch, sc in 2nd ch from hook and in each ch across, turn—36 sc.

Row 2: Ch 1 (bring ch to height of dc here and throughout), dc in first sc, sk next sc, trp-sh (see Stitch Guide) in next sc, *sk next 3 sc, trp-sh in next sc, rep from * to last 2 sc, sk next sc, dc in last sc, turn—8 trp-sh.

Row 3: Ch 1, dc in first dc, trp-sh in center ch-2 sp of each trp-sh across, leaving first and last ch-2 sps of each trp-sh unworked, dc in last dc, turn.

Rep Row 3 until piece measures 9" (23 cm). At end, change to A. Cont with Edging.

TRICOLOR WASHCLOTH

With B, ch 38 (or mult of 4 sts + 2).

Row 1: Working in bottom ridge lps of ch, sh (see Stitch Guide) in 2nd ch from hook, *sk next ch, dc in next ch, sk next ch, sh in next ch, rep from * across, change to C, turn — 10 sh, 9 dc.

Row 2: Ch 1, sh in ch-2 sp of first sh, *FPdc (see Stitch Guide) around next st, sh in ch-2 sp of next sh, rep from * across, turn—10 sh, 9 FPdc.

Rep Row 2 until piece measures 9½" (24 cm), following color order A-B-C to end. Cont with Edging.

EDGING
Solid washcloth only

Rnd 1: With A, ch 1, working in ch-2 sps from last row, row-ends, and free-lps from foundation row, sc evenly around, working 3 sc in each corner, sl st in first sc to join, change to C.

All washcloths

Next rnd: With C (striped or solid) or A (tricolor), ch 1, working in sts from last row, row-ends, and free-lps from foundation row, rsc (see Glossary) evenly around, working 3 rsc in each corner, sl st in first rsc to join.

Fasten off and weave in loose ends.

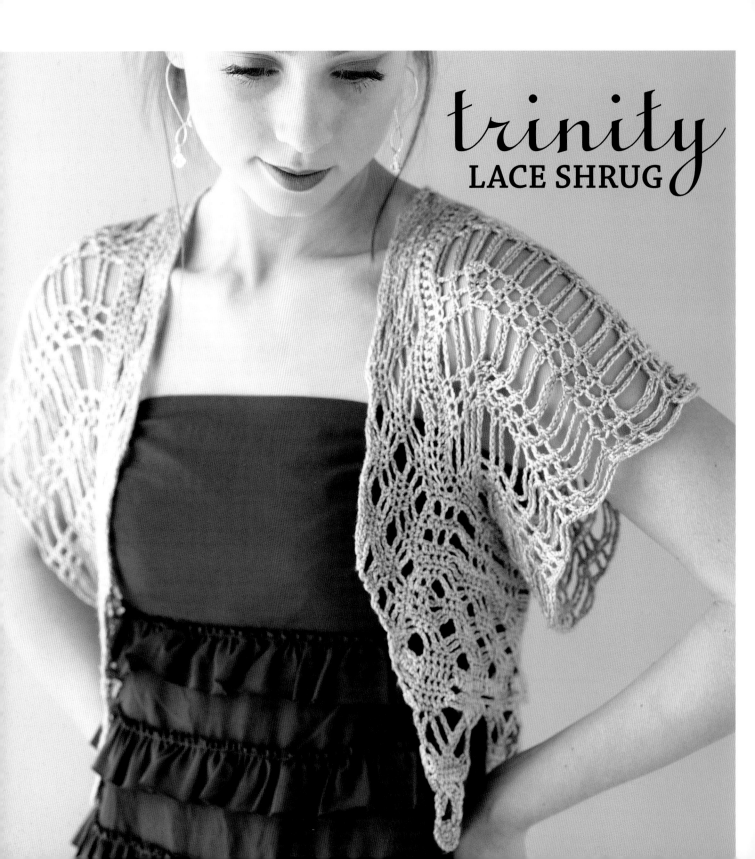

trinity
LACE SHRUG

S ometimes a shawl isn't structured enough, but a shrug is too casual. Leave it to Annie Modesitt to construct a shrug in intricate lace that's as formal as the most elegant of shawls and as practical as the coziest of shrugs. Paired with formal wear at a gala event or with a simple summer dress, this stunning garment is an heirloom-quality gift that will be worn over and over again.

FINISHED SIZE Size S (M, L, XL): 29 (37, 45, 53)" (73.5 [94, 114.5, 134.5] cm) bust circumference; to fit bust size 29 (37, 45, 53)" (73.5 [94, 114.5, 134.5] cm).

YARN Fingering weight (Super Fine #1), about 425 (550, 650, 775) yd (390 [510, 600, 725] m).

Shown here: Hand Maiden Sea Silk (70% silk, 30% SeaCell; 437 yd [400 m]/100 g) smoke, 1 (2, 2, 2) skeins.

HOOK Size F/5 (3.75 mm) crochet hook. Adjust hook size if necessary to obtain the correct gauge.

NOTIONS Stitch markers (m); safety pin; tapestry needle.

GAUGE 20 sts = 4" (10 cm) in sc.

NOTE
+ Unless specifically noted, each sc, hdc, dc, or ch counts as one stitch (st).

stitch guide

+ **TRINITY LACE PATTERN**

Row 1: (RS) Ch 2, hdc in next hdc, ch 3, sk 3 sc, sc in next 5 sc, *ch 5, sk 5 sc, sc in next 5 sc; rep from * across to last 3 sc, ch 3, sk 3 sc, hdc in last 2 hdc, turn.

Row 2: Ch 2, hdc in next hdc, *sc in next ch sp, ch 3, sk next sc, sc in next 3 sc, sk next sc, ch 3; rep from * ending with sc in last ch sp, hdc in last 2 hdc, turn.

Row 3: Ch 2, hdc in next hdc, sc in next sc, *sc in next ch sp, ch 3, sk next sc, sc in next sc, sk next sc, ch 3, sc in next ch sp, sc in next sc; rep from * ending with hdc in last 2 hdc, turn.

Row 4: Ch 2, hdc in next hdc, sc in next 2 sc, sc in next ch sp, *ch 5, sk next sc, sc in next (ch sp, 3 sc, ch sp); rep from * ending with sc in next (ch sp, 2 sc), hdc in last 2 hdc, turn.

Row 5: Ch 2, hdc in next hdc, sc in next 2 sc, *sk next sc, ch 3, sc in next ch sp, ch 3, sk next sc, sc in next 3 sc; rep from * ending with sc in last 2 sc, hdc in last 2 hdc, turn.

Row 6: Ch 2, hdc in next hdc, *sc in next sc, sk next sc, ch 3, sc in next (ch sp, sc, ch sp), ch 3, sk next sc; rep from * ending with ch 3, sc in last sc, hdc in last 2 hdc, turn.

Row 7: Ch 2, hdc in next hdc, ch 3, *sk next sc, sc in next (ch sp, 3 sc, ch sp), ch 5; rep from * ending ch 3, hdc in each of last 2 hdc, turn.

Rep Rows 2–7 for pattern.

+ **UNEVEN PARALLEL LACE PATTERN**

Row 1 (RS) Ch 2, hdc in next hdc, dc in next sc, ch 1, sk next st, dc in next st, *ch 5, sk 5 sts, dc in next st, [ch 1, sk next st, dc in next st] 2 times; rep from * to last 2 hdc, hdc in last 2 hdc, turn.

Row 2 Ch 2, hdc in next hdc, sc in each of next (dc, ch sp, dc), *ch 5, [sc in next dc, sc in next ch sp] 2 times, sc in next dc; rep from * ending with sc in next (dc, ch sp, dc), hdc in last 2 hdc, turn.

Rep Rows 1 and 2 for patt.

LOWER EDGE
Medallions (make 7 [9, 11, 13])

Make an adjustable ring, 9 sc in ring; do not join.

Set-up rnd: (RS) [Sc in next sc, ch 1] 9 times, sl st in first sc to join.

Row 1: (WS) Ch 1, hdc in first sc, ch 2, sk sc, sc in next ch, sk sc, ch 2, hdc in next sc, turn.

Row 2: Ch 1, hdc in first hdc, ch 7, hdc in last hdc, turn.

Row 3: Ch 1, hdc in first hdc, ch 4, sc in next ch sp, ch 4, hdc in last hdc, turn.

Row 4: Ch 1, hdc in first hdc, ch 4, sc in next ch sp, sc in next sc, sc in next ch sp, ch 4, hdc in last dc, turn.

Row 5: Ch 1, hdc in first dc, ch 4, sc in next ch sp, sc in next 3 sc, sc in next ch sp, ch 4, hdc in last hdc, turn.

Row 6: Ch 1, hdc in first dc, ch 4, sc in next ch sp, sc in next 5 sc, sc in next ch sp, ch 4, hdc in last hdc, turn.

Row 7: Ch 1, hdc in first hdc, ch 5, sk first sc, sc in next 5 sc, sk next sc, ch 5, hdc in last hdc, turn.

Row 8: Ch 1, hdc in first hdc, ch 7, sk first sc, sc in next 3 sc, sk next sc, ch 7, hdc in last hdc, turn.

Row 9: Ch 1, hdc in first hdc, ch 4, sc in next ch sp, ch 4, sk first sc, sc in next st, sk next sc, ch 4, sc in next ch sp, ch 4, hdc in last hdc, turn.

Row 10: Ch 1, hdc in first hdc, ch 4, sc in next ch sp, sc in next sc, sc in next ch sp, ch 7, sk next sc, sc in next ch sp, sc in next sc, sc in next ch sp, ch 4, hdc in last hdc, fasten off.

Lace Edge

Line up all 7 (9, 11, 13) medallions with RS facing and join all medallions as foll, starting with first medallion:

Row 1: (WS) 2 hdc in first hdc, ch 3, sc in next ch sp, sc in next 3 sc, (sc, ch 5, sc) in next ch sp, sc in next 3 sc, (sc, ch 3) in next ch sp, sc in next hdc, ch 1, move to next medallion, *sc in first hdc, ch 3, sc in next ch sp, sc in next 3 sc, (sc, ch 5, sc) in next ch sp, sc in next 3 sc**, (sc, ch 3) in next ch sp, sc in next hdc, ch 1, move to next medallion; rep from * for rem medallions, ending last medallion at **, sc in next ch sp, ch 3, 2 hdc in last hdc, turn.

Row 2: Ch 2 (counts as hdc here and throughout), hdc in next hdc, ch 3, *[sc in next 5 sc, ch 5] 2 times, sk (ch 3, sc, ch-1 sp, sc, ch 3); rep from * across ending last rep with ch 3, hdc in last 2 hdc, turn.

Row 3: Ch 2, hdc in next dc, 3 hdc in first ch sp, *hdc in

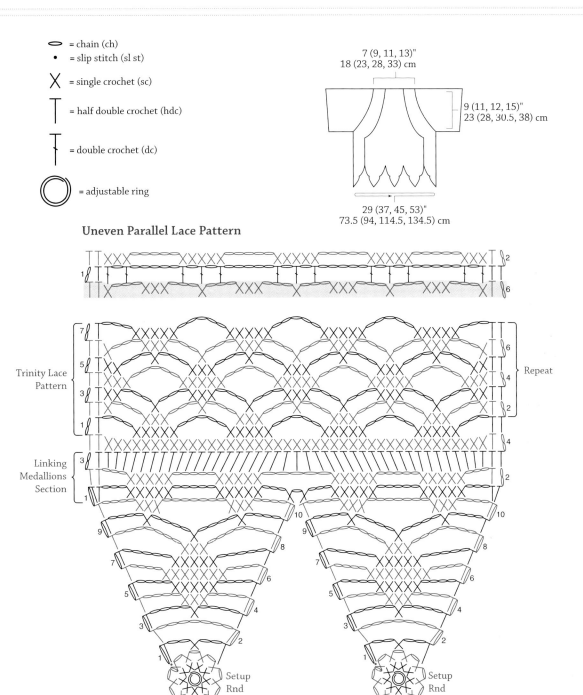

= chain (ch)

= slip stitch (sl st)

X = single crochet (sc)

T = half double crochet (hdc)

T = double crochet (dc)

= adjustable ring

7 (9, 11, 13)"
18 (23, 28, 33) cm

9 (11, 12, 15)"
23 (28, 30.5, 38) cm

29 (37, 45, 53)"
73.5 (94, 114.5, 134.5) cm

Uneven Parallel Lace Pattern

Trinity Lace Pattern

Repeat

Linking Medallions Section

Setup Rnd

Setup Rnd

Medallion

Medallion

next 5 sc, 5 hdc in ch sp; rep from * across ending with 3 hdc in last ch sp, hdc in last 2 hdc—145 (185, 225, 265) hdc.

Row 4: Ch 2, hdc in next hdc, sc in each hdc to last 2 hdc, hdc in last 2 hdc, turn.

Work trinity lace pattern (see Stitch Guide) for 18 rows, ending with Row 6.

Work uneven parallel lace pattern (see Stitch Guide) for 4 rows.

BODY SHAPING

Work short rows as foll: (*Note:* Each sc, hdc, dc, or ch counts as 1 st.)

Row 1: (RS) Work across 80 (110, 120, 150) sts in est patt ending with ch-5, work RS short-row shaping as foll: dc in next sc, ch 1, sk next sc, sc in next sc, sl st in next sc, turn.

Row 2: (WS) Sc in next (sc, ch, and dc), cont in est patt over next 15 sts, ending with ch-5, work WS short-row shaping as foll: sc in next 3 sc, sl st in next sc, turn.

Row 3: Ch 1, sc in next sc, ch 1, sk next sc, dc in next sc, cont in est patt, working 10 sts past prev RS short-row shaping, ending with ch-5, rep RS short-row shaping as for Row 1, turn.

Row 4: Sc in next (sc, ch, and dc), cont in est patt, working 10 sts past previous WS short-row shaping, ending with ch-5, rep WS short-row shaping as for Row 2, turn.

Work Rows 3–4 of Body Shaping 5 (7, 9, 11) more times to work each "ladder" section.

Work Row 1 of Uneven Parallel Lace patt, place safety pin in last st. Work Row 2 of Uneven Parallel Lace patt.

BEGIN BACK

Row 1: (RS) Work 90 (115, 140, 165) sts in est patt, hdc in next st, place marker (pm) in last st, turn.

Next row: (WS) Ch 2, cont in est patt across next 35 (45, 55, 65) sts, hdc in next st, pm in last st, turn.

Cont working these 37 (47, 57, 67) sts (Center Back sts) in patt as established for a total of 14 (18, 22, 26) rows, ending with a WS row. Fasten off.

ARMHOLE

With WS facing, join yarn at m at lower-left back "corner" (point where back began), do not remove m. Work 15 (20, 20, 25) sc evenly along row ends of back to top of back, ch 40 (55, 55, 70), sl st in st marked with safety pin (left armhole formed), do not remove pin. Cont across bottom edge of armhole toward first m, dec as foll: sc in next 8 (0, 3, 5) sts, [sc2tog (see Glossary) over next 2 sts] 20 (35, 40, 45) times, sc in next 7 (0, 2, 5) sts—35 (35, 45, 55) sc rem along bottom armhole edge. Sc to first m, sl st in first sc to join—90 (110, 120, 150) sts.

LEFT SLEEVE

The lace patt used in the sleeve is similar to the uneven parallel lace used in the body except ch-5 sps are replaced with ch-7 sps.

Rnd 1: Turn work so RS is facing, ch 1, [sc in next 5 sts, ch 7, sk 5 sc] 9 (11, 12, 15) times, sl st in first sc to join.

Rnd 2: Ch 3 (counts as dc here and throughout), [ch 1, sk next sc, dc in next st] 2 times, *ch 7, dc in next sc, [ch 1, sk next sc, dc in next st] 2 times; rep from * around, sl st in beg ch-3 to join.

Rnd 3: Ch 1, sc in first dc, [sc in next ch sp, sc in next dc] 2 times, ch 7, *[sc in next dc, sc in next ch sp] 2 times, sc in next dc, ch 7; rep from * around, sl st in first sc to join.

Rep Rnds 2–3 once, then work in patt as established to beg of 5-sc section closest to the top of sleeve. Beg 6-row short-row repeat as foll:

Row 1: (RS) Ch 3, [ch 1, sk next sc, dc in next st] 2 times, ch 7, dc in next sc, ch 1, sk next sc, sl st in next sc, turn.

Row 2: (WS) Sk sl st, sc in next ch-1 sp, sc in next dc, ch 7, [sc in next dc, sc in next ch sp] 2 times, sc in next dc,

ch 7, sc in next dc, sc in next ch sp, sl st in next sc, turn.

Row 3: Sk sl st, ch 1, sk next sc, dc in next sc (last st of 5-st section at center top), ch 7, [dc in next sc, ch 1, sk next sc] 2 times, sl st in next sc, turn.

Row 4: Sk sl st, [sc in next ch-1 sp, sc in next dc] 2 times, ch 7, [sc in next dc, sc in next ch sp] 2 times, sc in next dc, ch 7, [sc in next dc, sc in next ch sp] 2 times, sl st in next sc, turn.

Row 5: Sk sl st, [ch 1, sk next sc, dc in next sc] 2 times, ch 7, [dc in next sc, ch 1, sk next sc] 2 times, dc in next st, ch 7, sl st in next sc (first st of next 5-st section at center top), turn.

Row 6: Sk sl st, [ch 7, (sc in next dc, sc in next ch sp) 2 times, sc in next dc] 2 times, ch 7, sl st in next sc, turn.

Rep Rows 1–6, working out one more 5-st section from center top of sleeve with each 6-row repeat, until you have reached the last 5-st section before the markers. Note start of bottom armhole edge.

Turn work so RS is facing and work in uneven parallel patt established by first 2 rows of sleeve. Continue, working a total of 14 repeats of uneven parallel lace from top of sleeve cap or to desired sleeve length. Fasten off.

RIGHT SLEEVE

Note: By working the Right Sleeve with WS facing, the sleeve shaping can be worked exactly as for Left Sleeve.

Place markers at Right Back and Front corresponding to markers on left side. With WS facing, work as for Left Sleeve.

NECK

Join yarn at lower-left front edge just above lace medallion, work 25 (35, 35, 40) sc evenly along edge of trinity lace border.

Continue, working 40 (55, 55, 70) sc evenly along neck edge to back sts. Work across 35 (45, 55, 65) upper-back sts as foll: *ch 5, 5 sc into "ladder" portion of est back patt; rep from * to end of back, matching existing back patt.

Work 65 (90, 90, 110) sc evenly down right-front edge as for left-front edge, turn—165 (225, 235, 285) sts. Sc up right front to back, then begin working Row 2 of trinity lace patt as est across back. At left front, continue working in trinity lace patt as established at back to bottom-left front edge, turn.

Beginning with Row 3 of trinity lace patt, work up left front, working first 2 sts in row tog. Cont in trinity lace across back, then cont down right front in trinity lace patt as est at back.

With trinity lace patt est across neckline, cont working in lace as est for a total of 15 rows or to desired band length and *at the same time* work the first 2 sts of each row tog, adjusting the patt to omit these sts at the start of each row. Fasten off.

FINISHING

Weave in loose ends. Steam block to measurements, opening the lace up as fully as possible.

fossil
NECKWARMER

The pattern this yarn creates when simply stitched in circles reminds designer Kathy Merrick of the traces of ancient creatures left behind in rocks. The yarn's softness feels wonderful against the sensitive skin of the neck. A quick and handy gift with style.

FINISHED SIZE 24¼" (61.5 cm) circumference and 9½" (24 cm) from top to bottom, measured after blocking.

YARN Bulky weight (Bulky #5), 196 yd (179 m).

Shown here: DiVé Autunno (100% extrafine Merino wool; 98 yd [90 m]/ 50 g): pink mix #14627, 2 balls.

HOOK Size K/10.5 (6.5mm). Adjust hook size if necessary to obtain the correct gauge.

NOTIONS Removable stitch marker (m); tapestry needle.

GAUGE Large motif = 4¾" (12 cm) diameter, measured after blocking.

NOTES

+ Work motifs in spiral fashion; do not join rounds with slip stitch.

+ Place marker (pm) at beginning of round, then move the marker up as work progresses.

First Motif

Rnd 1: Ch 3 (counts as hdc here and throughout), 7 hdc in 3rd ch from hook, do not join, place marker (pm) in first st to mark beg of rnd (see Notes)—8 hdc.

Rnd 2: 2 hdc in each hdc around—16 hdc.

Rnd 3: Hdc in each hdc around.

Rnd 4: Rep Rnd 2—32 hdc.

Rnds 5–6: Rep Rnd 3. Fasten off.

Remaining Motifs

Work as for first motif except on Rnd 6, join motif to previous motif as foll: [hdc, sl st in corresponding st on previous motif] 4 times, complete rnd as established. Fasten off.

FIRST RND OF NECKWARMER

Make and join 5 motifs, joining last motif to first motif to form a ring.

SECOND RND OF NECKWARMER

Make and join 5 motifs as foll: join one side to previous motif over 4 sts, sk next 4 sts, join working motif to corresponding motif on previous rnd over next 4 sts, making sure to skip 4 sts from existing join on corresponding motif as well.

Into skipped space between motifs, work small motif as foll:

Rnd 1: Ch 3 (counts as hdc), 7 hdc in 3rd ch from hook—8 hdc.

Rnd 2: [Hdc in next st, sl st in first skipped st of large motif, hdc in same st of working motif, sl st in next skipped st of large motif] 2 times to join each side of small motif to each of the 4 adjoining larger motifs—16 sts. Fasten off.

EDGING

Join yarn to center st of one of top-rnd motifs, *sc in next 3 sts, 2 sc in next st; rep from * around top edge, working sc in each join. Fasten off. Rep for lower edge of neckwarmer.

FINISHING

Weave in loose ends. Steam gently to shape.

ravissant

SOCKS

a lacy stitch pattern and picot hem add a bit of romance to these cozy socks. Crocheted from the toe up and designed with the vision of relaxing next to a fire with a cup a tea in hand, they're sure to become favorites. And when they do become favorites, the heels can be replaced at the first sign of stress: just rip them out and re-crochet.

FINISHED SIZE S (M, L); 7¼ (8⅛, 9)" (18.5 [20.5, 23] cm) circumference at ball of foot.

YARN Fingering weight (Super Fine #1), about 385 (430, 500) yd (352 [393, 457] m).

Shown here: Lorna's Laces Shepherd Sock (80% superwash wool, 20% nylon; 215 yd [196 m]/2 oz): periwinkle 46ns, 2 (2, 3) hanks.

HOOK Size E/4 (3.5 mm). Adjust hook size if necessary to obtain the correct gauge.

NOTIONS 4 stitch markers (m); tapestry needle.

GAUGE 24 sts and 20 rows = 4" (10 cm) in esc (see Stitch Guide) after blocking.

5 V-sts and 16 rows = 4" (10 cm) in lace pattern (see Stitch Guide) after blocking.

NOTES

+ Stitch pattern and yarn have substantial give; choose foot circumference that is slightly smaller than recipient's foot circumference for snug socks.

+ On rnds where markers (m) are not used, move them up as work progresses.

+ Sock is worked from toe up with an afterthought heel that can be replaced at any time.

stitch guide

+ EXTENDED SINGLE CROCHET (ESC)
Insert hook in st and pull up lp, yo and draw through 1 lp on hook, yo and draw through 2 lps on hook.

+ V-ST
(Dc, ch 2, dc) in same st or sp.

+ 2V-ST
(2 dc, ch 2, 2 dc) in same st.

+ LACE PATTERN (mult of 6 sts + 2)
Ch 32.

Row 1: (RS) Sc in 2nd ch from hook, *sk 2 ch, 2V-St (see above) in next ch, sk 2 ch, sc in next ch; rep from * to end, turn—five 2V-Sts.

Row 2: Ch 3 (counts as first dc), dc in same sc, ch 1, sc in next ch-2 sp, *ch 1, V-St (see above) in next sc, ch 1, sc in next ch-2 sp; rep from * to last sc, ch 1, 2 dc in last sc, turn.

Row3: Ch 1, sc in first dc, *2V-st in next sc, sc in next ch-2 sp; rep from * to last sc, 2V-st in last sc, sc in last dc, turn.

Rep Rows 2–3 for patt.

TOE

Ch 8 (9, 10).

Rnd 1: (RS) Esc (see Stitch Guide) in third ch from hook (skipped ch count as first esc), place marker (pm) in st just made, esc in each ch to last ch, 3 esc in last ch, pm in first and third esc just made, turn work 180 degrees to work in opposite side of foundation ch, esc in next 5 (6, 7) ch, pm in last esc, sl st in top of tch to join, turn—14 (16, 18) esc.

Rnd 2: Ch 2 (counts as first esc here and throughout), 2 esc in next st, pm in 2nd esc just made, esc to next m, 2 esc in next st, pm in first esc just made, esc in next st, 2 esc in next st, pm in 2nd esc just made, esc to next m, 2 esc in last st, pm in first esc just made, sl st in tch to join, turn—18 (20, 22) esc.

Rnd 3: Ch 2, esc in next st, pm in st just made, 2 esc in next esc, esc to next m, 2 esc in marked st, esc in next st, pm in st just made, esc to next m, pm in st made before marked st, 2 esc in marked st, esc to next m, 2 esc in marked st, esc in next st, pm in st just made, esc in next st, sl st in tch to join, turn—22 (24, 26) esc. Rep Rnds 2–3 two (three, three) more times—38 (48, 50) esc.

Sizes S and L only

Next rnd: Rep Rnd 2, sl st in next 2 (5) sts, turn.

Size M only

Next rnd: Ch 2, esc in next st and in each st around, sl st in next 3 sts, turn.

Arch Increase

Rnd 1: (RS): Ch 1, sc in first sl st, *sk 2 sts, 2V-st (see Stitch Guide) in next st, sk 2 sts, sc in next st; rep from * 3 (4, 5) more times, esc in next 8 esc, 3 esc in next esc, pm in first and third esc just made, esc to end, sl st in first sc to join, turn—4 (5, 6) 2V-st + 19 esc.

Rnd 2: Ch 3 (counts as dc), esc in each esc across, 2 dc in next sc, ch 1, sc in next ch-2 sp, *ch 1, V-st (see Stitch Guide) in next sc, ch 1, sc in next ch-2 sp; rep from * to last ch-2 sp, ch 1, dc in last sc, sl st in tch to join, turn.

Rnd 3: Ch 1, sc in first dc, *2V-st in next sc, sc in next ch-2 sp; rep from * to last sc, 2V-st in last sc, sc in last dc, esc in each esc to end, sl st in first sc to join, turn.

Rnd 4: Ch 3 (counts as dc), esc in each esc to next m, 2 esc in marked st, pm in first esc just made, esc to next m, 2 esc in marked st, pm in 2nd esc just made, esc in each esc across, 2 dc in next sc, ch 1, sc in next ch-2 sp, *ch 1, V-st in next sc, ch 1, sc in next ch-2 sp; rep from * to last ch-2 sp, ch 1, dc in last sc, sl st in tch to join, turn—21 esc.

Rnds 5–8: Rep Rnd 3, then Rnds 2–4—23 esc.

Rnds 9–10: Rep Rnd 3, then Rnd 2.

Rnd 11: Ch 1, sc in first dc, *2V-st in next sc, sc in next ch-2 sp; rep from * to last sc, 2V-st in last sc, sc in last dc, esc in each esc to next m, 2 esc in next st, pm in first esc just made, esc in each esc to next m, 2 esc in next st, pm in 2nd esc just made, esc in each esc across, sl st in first sc to join, turn—25 esc.

Rep Rnds 2–3, then Rnd 2, then Rnd 11—27 esc.

Rep Rnds 2–4—29 esc.

Rep Rnd 3, then Rnds 2–4—31 esc.

Rep Rnd 3.

Sizes M and L only

Rep Rnd 2, then Rnd 11—33 esc.

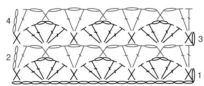

Reduced sample of lace pattern

⬭ = chain (ch)

✕ = single crochet (sc)

🇹 = double crochet (dc)

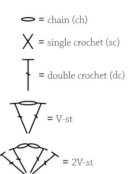 = V-st

= 2V-st

Size L only

Rep Rnds 2–3, then Rnd 2, then Rnd 11—35 esc.

All sizes

Last Rnd: Ch 32 (32, 38) for heel opening, sk all esc, 2 dc in next sc, ch 1, sc in next ch-2 sp, *ch 1, V-St in next sc, ch 1, sc in next ch-2 sp; rep from * to last ch-2 sp, ch 1, dc in last sc, sl st in 3rd ch of beg ch to join, turn. Do not fasten off; cont with cuff.

CUFF

Rnd 1: (RS) Ch 1, sc in sl st, *2V-st in next sc, sc in next ch-2 sp; rep from * to last sc, 2V-st in last sc, sc in last dc, **sk 2 ch, 2V-st in next ch, sk 2 ch, sc in next ch; rep from ** to last 5 ch, sk 2 ch, 2V-st in next ch, sk 2 ch, sl st in first sc to join, turn—9 (10, 12) 2V-sts.

Rnd 2: Ch 4 (counts as dc, ch-1), sc in next ch-2 sp, *ch 1, V-st in next sc, ch 1, sc in next ch-2 sp; rep from * to last ch-2 sp, ch 1, dc in last sc, hdc in 3rd ch of tch to join, turn.

Rnd 3: Ch 1, sc in sp made by hdc, *2V-st in next sc, sc in next ch-2 sp; rep from * to last sc, 2V-st in last sc, sl st in first sc to join, turn.

Rnds 4–25: Rep Rnds 2–3 eleven more times.

Rnd 26: Rep Rnd 2.

Rnd 27: Ch 1, sc in sp made by hdc, *sc in next ch-1 sp, sc in next sc, sc in next ch-1 sp, 3 sc in next ch-2 sp, rep from * to hdc, 2 sc in sp made by hdc, sl st in first sc to join, turn—54 (60, 72) sc.

Rnd 28: Ch 1, sc in each sc around, sl st in first sc to join, turn.

Rnd 29: Ch 1, *sc in next sc, ch 3, sl st in first ch to form picot, sc in next sc, ch 2, sk 1 sc; rep from * around, sl st in first sc to join, fasten off and weave in loose ends.

HEEL

With RS facing, join yarn with sl st at start of the heel opening in the 2nd ch of the tch.

Rnd 1: (RS) Ch 1, sc in tch, pm in sc just made, sc in next esc and each esc across, 2 sc around post of next dc, pm in first sc just made, sc in next ch and each ch across lace patt, sc once more in tch, sl st in first sc, sl st in next sc, turn—68 (68, 74) sc.

Rnd 2: Ch 1, sc3tog (see Glossary) over (next 2 sl sts and next sc), sc in each sc to 1 st before m, sc3tog over next 3 sc, pm in sc3tog just made, sc to end, sl st to first sc, sl st in next sc, turn—64 (64, 70) sc.

Rep Rnd 2 thirteen (thirteen, fifteen) times.

Turn sock inside out, sl st through both sides of fabric across heel, fasten off, and weave in loose ends.

FINISHING

Handwash socks in gentle wool wash, block to desired size, and allow to dry.

flower
CHOKER

This delicate, feminine choker was designed with bridesmaids' gifts in mind. To calm her nerves and keep her hands busy as the big day approaches, the soon-to-be blushing bride can crochet these relatively quick necklaces for each woman in her bridal party to coordinate with their dresses. Playing with color would result in a lovely choker suitable for less formal occasions.

FINISHED SIZE AND SIZING
Neck strap, 20½" (52 cm) neck circumference; flower, 2½" (6.5 cm) diameter.

YARN Size 10 crochet thread (Lace #0), 25–50 yd (23–46 m) in each of 3 colors.

Shown here: Aunt Lydia's Fashion Crochet Thread Size 10 (100% cotton; 350 yd [320 m]/skein: French Rose #0493, Orchid Pink #0401, and Frosty Green #0661, 1 skein each.

HOOK Size 7 (1.65 mm) steel hook. Adjust hook size if necessary to obtain correct gauge.

NOTIONS Small-eye tapestry needle.

GAUGE 36 sts and 48 rows = 4" (10 cm) in sc.

CHOKER
Flower
With A, ch 11, sl st in first ch to form a ring.

Rnd 1: Ch 10, sk first 2 ch of ring, dc in next ch, *ch 8, sk next ch, dc in next ch; rep from * 2 more times, ch 8, sl st in 2nd ch of beg ch-10 to join—5 ch-sps.

Rnd 2: Ch 1, *7 sc in next ch-sp, sc in next dc; rep from * 3 times, 7 sc in next ch-sp, sc in beg ch-1 to join.

Rnd 3: *Ch 3, 2 dc in each of next 7 sc, ch 3, sl st in next sc; rep from * around ending with sl st in base of beg ch-3 to join.

Rnd 4: Ch 1, sc in next ch-3 sp, *ch 3, [dc in next dc, ch 1] 14 times, [sc in next ch-3 sp] twice; rep from * 4 times, omitting final sc.

Rnd 5: *Sc in next sc, (4 dc, sc) in next ch-3 sp, [(sc, 4 dc, sc) in next ch-1 sp] 13 times, sk next dc, sc in next sc; rep from * around, sl st in beg sc to join. Fasten off.

Flower Center
With B and leaving a long tail, beg with slip knot on hook. Wrap tail around first finger of your non-working hand to form a ring.

Rnd 1: 10 sc in ring, pull tail to close ring, sl st in first sc to join—10 sc.

Rnd 2: Ch 1, 2 sc in each sc around, sl st in first sc to join—20 sc.

Rnd 3: Ch 1, 2 sc in first sc, sc in next sc, *2 sc in next sc, sc in next sc; rep from * around, sl st in first sc to join—30 sc.

Rnd 4: Ch 1, sc in each sc around, sl st in first sc to join.

Rnds 5–7: Rep Rnd 4.

Rnd 8: Ch 1, sc in first 2 sc, sk next sc, *sc in next 2 sc, sk next sc; rep from * around, sl st in first sc to join—20 sc.

Rnd 9: Rep Rnd 8—14 sc. Fasten off, leaving a tail long enough for sewing.

Leaf
With C, ch 15.

Rnd 1: Sc in bottom ridge lp of 2nd ch from hook, sc in next ch, hdc in next 2 ch, dc in next 6 ch, tr in next 3 ch, 8 tr in last ch, working up other side in the unworked lps of ch, tr in next 3 ch, dc in next 6 ch, hdc in next 2 ch, sc in next 2 ch.

Rnd 2: Ch 2, sc in each st around, sl st in first ch of beg ch-2. Fasten off.

Neck strap
With C, ch 185.

Row 1: Sc in 2nd ch from hook, sc in each ch across, turn—184 sc.

Row 2: Ch 1, sc in each sc across, turn.

Rows 3–6: Rep Row 2.

FINISHING
With tapestry needle and matching thread, sew flower center to inside of flower, sew leaf to back of flower, sew flower to neck strap 12" (30.5 cm) from one end. Weave in loose ends.

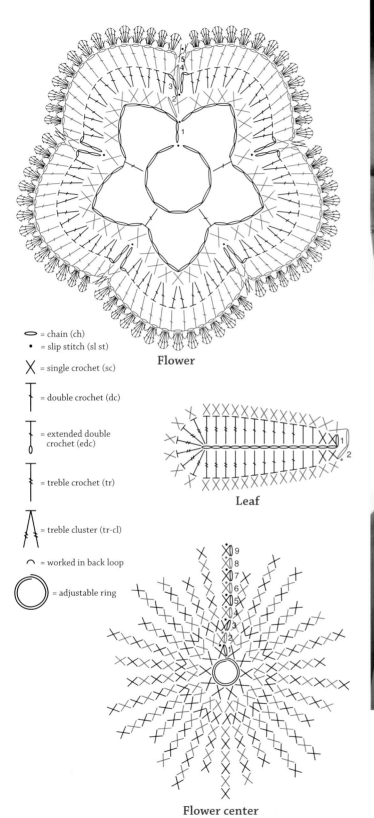

Flower

Leaf

= chain (ch)

• = slip stitch (sl st)

✕ = single crochet (sc)

= double crochet (dc)

= extended double crochet (edc)

= treble crochet (tr)

= treble cluster (tr-cl)

⌢ = worked in back loop

○ = adjustable ring

Flower center

hex zipper
BAG

*C*onstruct a flat shape out of hexagonal motifs, and with a few seams, it becomes three-dimensional. Benefitting from a sturdy yarn, a fabric lining, and a zipper closure, the shape makes a useful little bag for storing makeup, jewelry, pens, or anything else. Make each motif in a different color and you can use up stash yarn in a creative way for a quick gift appropriate for nearly any occasion.

FINISHED SIZE 3¾" (9.5 cm) tall, 9½" (24 cm) wide, and 4" (10 cm) deep.

YARN DK weight (Light #3), about 60 yd (55 m) in main color 50 yd (46 m) each in 2 contrast colors.

Shown here: Hemp for Knitting Allhemp6 Lux (100% hemp, 143 yds [130 m]/100 g): zinfandel #52 (red; A), ice #57 (blue; B), and roux #58 (ecru; C), 1 skein each.

HOOK Size F/5 (3.75 mm). Adjust hook size if necessary to obtain the correct gauge.

NOTIONS Tapestry needle; 9" (23 cm) zipper; ½ yd [.5 m] double-sided lining fabric; sewing needle and matching thread; fabric glue (optional).

GAUGE Hexagon motif = 3½" (9 cm) side to side; 4" (10 cm) point to point.

NOTES
+ Hexagon motifs are made separately, then joined.

+ Seams are sewn at the sides, which gives the flat piece its three-dimensional shape.

+ Choose lining fabric that has no wrong side, as both sides of the fabric will show.

+ HEXAGON
Ch 6, sl st in first ch to form ring.

Rnd 1: Ch 3 (counts as dc), 2 dc in ring, [ch 2, 3 dc in ring] 5 times, ch 2, sl st in top of beg ch-3 to join—6 ch-2 sps.

Rnd 2: [Sl st in next dc] twice, sl st in next ch-2 sp, ch 4 (counts as tr), (2 tr, ch 2, 3 tr) in same sp, *(3 tr, ch 2, 3 tr) in next ch-2 sp; rep from * 4 times, sl st in top of beg ch-4 to join.

Rnd 3: Ch 1, sc in each tr and (sc, ch 1, sc) in each ch-2 sp around, sl st in beg ch-1 to join. Fasten off.

+ HALF-HEXAGON— Ch 6, sl st in first ch to form ring.

Row 1: Ch 5 (counts as dc, ch 2), (3 dc, ch 2) three times in ring, dc in ring, turn—4 ch-2 sps.

Rnd 2: Ch 6 (counts as tr, ch 2), 3 tr in next ch-2 sp, [(3 tr, ch 2, 3 tr) in next ch-2 sp] 2 times, (3 tr, ch 2, tr) in top ch-2 of ch-5, turn.

Rnd 3: Ch 1, sc in next ch-2 sp, *sc in next 3 tr, (sc, ch 1, sc) in next ch-2 sp; rep from * 2 times ending with (sc, ch 1, sl st) in top of ch-6. Fasten off.

BAG

Following Hexagon Motif diagram at right and using colors as indicated in diagram below right, start at one corner making hexagons (see Stitch Guide) and joining them on the last rnd at each ch-1 point by working (sc, ch 1, sl st in corresponding ch-1 sp of completed motif, sc). Make half-hexagons (see Stitch Guide) and join to piece.

Block piece to measurements.

With RS facing, seam bag according to seaming diagram below right. Whipstitch (see Glossary) back loops of each sc and ch on corresponding sides of motifs. Weave in loose ends, tacking down with fabric glue if necessary.

Hexagon Motif

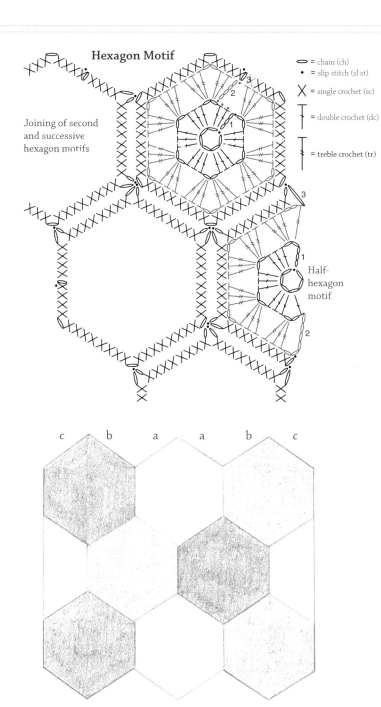

Joining of second and successive hexagon motifs

= chain (ch)

• = slip stitch (sl st)

X = single crochet (sc)

| = double crochet (dc)

‡ = treble crochet (tr)

Half-hexagon motif

Seam a's together. Seam b's together. Seam c's together.

FINISHING

Make lining as foll: Fold fabric in half with selvedges together. With fold facing you and positioning bottom of lining on fold of fabric, cut a rectangle on the fold that is 13¾" (35 cm) wide and 7½" (19 cm) long, which will unfold to 15" [38 cm] when laid flat. Sew side seams with French seam to hide all raw edges as foll: Fold fabric with WS tog. Seam ¼" (6 mm) in from raw edge along left side. Turn lining right side out, press along seam, and seam again ⅜" (1 cm) in from edge. With WS out, fold top seam down ¼" (6 mm) and press. Stitch around top edge. Rep for other side edge. Shape bottom of bag by folding ends in 2" (5 cm) at right angles to bottom fold as in lining diagram. Stitch 2" (5 cm) in from point. Rep at other corner. Tack the point to the bottom of the outside of the lining. At top edge, fold 1" (5 cm) overlap in center of the front and the back as in diagram, pin, and stitch. If fabric is too thick, you may also form two ½" (1.3 cm) folds evenly spaced along top edge to reduce the top edge of the bag by 2" (5 cm). Sew in zipper (see Glossary).

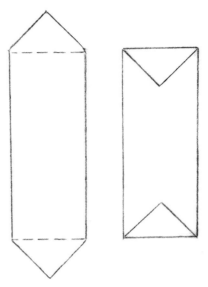

Fold points out and stitch. Tack the points to the underside of the bag.

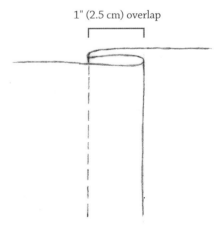

1" (2.5 cm) overlap

PLAY TIME

Sometimes small speaks volumes. These wee juggling balls or hacky sacks are easy—they're worked entirely in single crochet—and they're quick to stitch up. Since so little yarn is used, you can whip up a whole batch in a weekend or use up the random yards-long scraps you can't bear to throw away.

PATTERN

Note: Instructions are given for solid-color ball. Add striping, colorwork, and/or embellishment as you wish. Loop yarn tail behind working yarn to form an adjustable ring, insert hook in ring, yo and pull up lp.

Rnd 1: Ch 1, 8 sc in ring, place marker (pm) in last st to mark end of rnd (move m up as work progresses), pull yarn tail to tighten ring—8 sts.

Rnd 2: 2 sc in each st around—16 sts.

Rnd 3: [Sc in next st, 2 sc in next st] around—24 sts.

Rnd 4: [Sc in next 2 sts, 2 sc in next st] around—32 sts.

Rnds 5–10: Sc in each st around.

Rnd 11: [Sc2tog (see Glossary), sc in next 2 sts] around—24 sts rem. Beg stuffing ball with balloon and/or stuffing as needed (see Notes).

Rnd 12: [Sc2tog, sc in next st] around—16 sts rem.

Rnd 13: Sc2tog around—8 sts rem.

FINISHING

Cut yarn, leaving a 10" (25.5 cm) tail. With yarn needle, thread tail in and out of rem 8 sts and pull to cinch closed. Weave in loose ends.

FINISHED SIZE About 2½" (6.5 cm) in diameter.

YARN Worsted weight (Medium #4), about 10–15 yd (10–15 m) for each ball. *Shown here:* Patons SWS (70% wool, 30% soy; 110 yd [100 m]/2.8 oz [80 g]); tan 70012 and light blue 70129, 1 skein each.

HOOK Size H/8 (5.0 mm) crochet hook. Adjust hook size if necessary to obtain a firm fabric (see Notes).

NOTIONS Stitch marker (m); tapestry needle; small balloon; small amount of poly-fill or stuffing of your choice; rice or small dry beans.

GAUGE About 5 sts and 5 rows = 1" (2.5 cm) in sc.

NOTES + Ball is worked in spiral without joining rounds.

+ If desired, insert small balloon filled with rice or dried beans into ball before stuffing with poly-fill and closing up. Be sure to insert balloon and/or stuffing when hole is still large enough to accommodate it; finish remaining rows and fasten off after stuffing, topping up as needed as you work.

+ Gauge should be tight to prevent stuffing from coming through the stitches, but attaining exact gauge listed is not crucial.

HAT
squared

a soft, deep brown alpaca yarn, a simple stitch pattern, and a very straightforward bit of shaping result in a suitably masculine hat that's quick to stitch. Playing with color would be a sure way to create a gift for any recipient.

FINISHED SIZE 22" (56 cm) circumference at brim; 8½" (21.5 cm) from chain edge to top of hat.

YARN Sportweight (Fine #2), about 250 yd (229 m).

Shown here: Blue Sky Alpacas Sport Weight (100% baby alpaca; 110 yd [100 m]/50 g): dark brown #501, 3 skeins.

HOOK Size E/4 (3.5 mm). Adjust hook size if necessary to obtain the correct gauge.

NOTIONS Removable stitch marker (m); tapestry needle.

GAUGE 18 sts and 16 rows = 4" (10 cm) in hdc.

NOTES

+ Hat is worked in the round in spiral fashion; do not join rounds with slip stitch.

+ Place marker (m) in first stitch to mark beginning of round; move the marker up as work progresses.

71

HAT

Ch 100, sl st in first ch to form ring, being careful not to twist ch.

Rnd 1: Ch 2 (count as hdc), place marker (pm) in 2nd ch to mark beg of rnd (see Notes), hdc in next ch and in each ch around, do not join—100 hdc.

Rnd 2: Hdc in each hdc around.

Rep Rnd 2 until hat measures 6¼" (16 cm) from beg.

Shape crown

Rnd 1: [Hdc2tog (see Glossary) over next 2 sts, 23 hdc] 4 times—96 hdc.

Rnd 2: Work even in hdc.

Rnd 3: [Hdc2tog over next 2 sts, 22 hdc] 4 times—92 hdc.

Rnd 4: Work even in hdc.

Rnd 5: [Hdc2tog over next 2 sts, 21 hdc] 4 times—88 hdc.

Rnd 6: Work even in hdc.

Rnd 7: [Hdc2tog over next 2 sts, 20 hdc] 4 times—84 hdc.

Rnd 8: Work even in hdc.

Rnd 9: [Hdc2tog over next 2 sts, 19 hdc] 4 times—80 hdc.

Rnd 10: Work even in hdc.

FINISHING

Draw the 4 decrease points to center of hat and, with needle and yarn, sew a few sts to secure fabric at center, forming a "+" shape with four arms extending from the center. Fasten off.

Holding edges of one arm together, whipstitch (see Glossary) opening, working from one side of the "+" over the center stitches and across the opposite side. Fasten off.

Rep with remaining open edges. Fasten off. Weave in loose ends.

beaded
RING
felted
BAG

*I*nspired by her mother's love of beading and the long distance that separates them, designer Jill Wright designed the perfect little travel bag. The triangle ends and trapezoid sides are shaped in the round as you go, and a little bead-crochet ring adds the perfect finishing touch. You could even make a matching necklace and earrings.

FINISHED SIZE 14" (35.5 cm) wide, 7" (18 cm) deep, and 11" (28 cm) high before felting; 11" (28 cm) wide (7" [18 cm] wide at the top), 6" (15 cm) deep, and 8½" (21.5 cm) high after felting.

YARN Worsted-weight (Medium #4) wool (not superwash treated), about 370 yd [338 m] main color and 175 yd (160 m) contrast color.

Shown here: Brown Sheep Lamb's Pride (85% wool, 15% mohair, 190 yds [173 m]/4 oz): Limeade #M120 (green; A), 2 skeins, and Onyx #M-05 (black; B), 1 skein.

HOOK Size H/8 (5.0 mm). Adjust hook size if necessary to obtain the correct gauge.

NOTIONS 4 stitch markers (m); tapestry needle; 1 sheet plastic canvas; scissors; sewing needle; black sewing thread; 7" (18 cm) closed-end black zipper.

BEAD CROCHET MATERIALS Size 8 (1.5 mm) steel crochet hook; pearl cotton thread size #8; 316 size 8° opaque black seed beads (about 10 g); 158 size 8° clear silver-lined round-hole seed beads (about 5 g); large-eye beading needle.

GAUGE 12½ sts and 10 rows = 4" (10 cm) in hdc with yarn and larger hook, before felting.

NOTES

+ Base is worked as a flat rectangle. Stitches are picked up around the edge of the base, then strategic decreases form triangle ends and trapezoid front and back. Stitch markers (m) should be placed when picking up sts around the base to mark correct decrease placement.

+ Do not count first ch-1 in each row as a st.

+ Turn after every row unless instructed otherwise.

BASE

With A, ch 45.

Row 1: Working in bottom ridge lp of ch, hdc in 2nd ch from hook and in each ch across, turn—44 sts.

Rows 2–16: Ch 1, hdc in each st across, turn. Do not fasten off at the end of Row 16.

BODY

Beg working in joined rnds, turning after each rnd. Move markers up every row to mark position of decreases.

Rnd 1: Ch 1, hdc across, do not turn, cont around edge of base as foll: work 23 hdc evenly spaced across row ends, hdc in 44 unused lps of foundation ch, work 23 hdc evenly across row ends, sl st in beg ch-1 to join, turn—134 sts.

Rnd 2: Ch 1, *hdc in next 23 hdc, place marker (pm) in base of last st to mark corner, hdc in next 44 hdc, pm in base of last st; rep from * around, sl st in beg ch-1 to join, turn—4 corners marked.

Rnds 3–4: Ch 1, hdc in each st around, sl st in beg ch-1 to join, turn.

Rnd 5: Ch 1, hdc2tog (see Glossary), *hdc to 2 sts before next m, hdc2tog before and after m; rep from * to

2 sts before last m, hdc2tog, sl st in beg ch-1 to join, turn—8 sts dec'd.

Rnd 6: Ch 1, hdc in each st around, sl st in beg ch-1 to join, turn.

Rnds 7–8: Rep Rnds 5–6—118 sts.

Rnd 9: Ch 1, *hdc to m, hdc2tog after m, hdc across short end to 2 sts before next m, hdc2tog; rep from * once, sl st in beg ch-1 to join, turn—4 sts dec'd.

Rnd 10: Ch 1, hdc in each st around, sl st in beg ch-1 to join, turn.

Rnd 11–22: Rep Rnds 7–10 three times—78 hdc.

Rnd 23: Rep Rnd 5—70 hdc.

Rnd 24: Ch 1, hdc in next 32 sts, hdc3tog (see Glossary) over next 3 sts, hdc in next 32 sts, hdc3tog, sl st in beg ch-1 to join, turn—66 sts.

Rnd 25: Ch 1, hdc in each st around, sl st in beg ch-1 to join, change to color B, turn.

Rnds 26–29: With B, ch 1, hdc in each st around, sl st in beg ch-1 to join. Fasten off.

HANDLE AND PIPING CORD

With B, ch 5, sl st in first ch to form ring.

Rnd 1: Ch 1, hdc in each ch, do not join or turn—5 hdc.

Rnd 2: Hdc in each hdc around.

Cont in a spiral, working 5 sts in each rnd until cord measures 2½ yd (2.25 m). Tug regularly to seat sts comfortably but allow cord to relax before measuring. Fasten off and sew end to end to form large loop.

Decorative Loop

With B, work as for handle and piping cord for 10" (25.5 cm). Fasten off. (Do not sew short ends together yet.)

Following directions on page 77, work a bead crochet loop, but do not attach before felting (see page 78).

BEAD CROCHET LOOP

String beads onto thread as foll: [2 black, 1 silver]; rep until 42" (106.5 cm) of beads are strung.

Place slipknot on steel hook, [bring 1 bead snug to hook, yo and draw through lp on hook to form ch] 6 times. Ch forms a comma shape. Form circle with 6 bead ch, bring first bead ch to hook and place hook under thread just to left of bead. Push bead away so it stands upright behind hook. Thread should be in front of bead, not wrapped underneath **(Figure 1)**.

Figure 1

Bring next bead to hook (new bead should be same color as bead you are working into), hold in place behind hook, yo, pull thread through st and lp (beaded sl st). Cont in beaded sl st **(Figure 2)** to end of strung beads. Sl st without beads to make last rnd of beads stand up. Beads should stand upright once worked; colors will spiral around cord. Fasten off, leaving an 8" (20.5 cm) tail. Do not weave in end.

Figure 2

FINISHING

With yarn needle and gently stretching piping cord, backstitch (see Glossary) through 1 layer of piping only to allow piping to stand proud of bag. Stitch piping down dec line toward front of bag, under bag along short end, and up other side's dec line, ending stitching before entering contrast color. Lay piping along B at the top with a little slack to form short handle. Beg stitching again down dec line on opposite edge, under bag, and up other side, ending stitching before entering contrast color. Rem lp forms long handle on front of bag.

Stitch decorative lp end to end around short strap to form a chain.

FELTING

Place bag in mesh laundry bag or pillowcase. Set washing machine to hot wash, cold rinse, longest cycle. Add small amount of wool-friendly detergent. Add bag plus 1 pair of well-washed jeans to the washer (do not put in beaded ring). Run wash cycle until bag has felted to desired size. (You may remove bag to check size during wash cycle.) Remove and squeeze out excess water; do not allow to spin. Rinse by hand, squeeze out excess water. Pull to shape and stuff with plastic bags if desired to hold shape. Allow to air-dry.

Flip short decorative strap to front of bag and thread bead crochet loop through decorative loop. Using beading needle, stitch bead crochet loop end to end to form a chain. Cut plastic canvas to size, cut rounded corners, and insert in base of bag.

Sew in zipper (see Glossary).

FLORAL COASTERS

Bits of yarn are well used when stitched into coasters that make great housewarming or hostess gifts. Here are two options, but imagine what possibilities exist in the infinite varieties of crochet motifs.

MOORISH MEDALLION (four-pointed flower)

Ch 4, sl st in first ch to form ring.

Rnd 1: Ch 1, 16 sc in center of ring, sl st in first sc to join—16 sts.

Rnd 2: Ch 1, sc first 2 sc, *(sc, ch 9, sc) in next sc, sc in next 3 sc; rep from * 3 times omitting final 2 sc on last rep, sl st in first sc to join.

Rnd 3: Ch 1, sc in first sc, sk next sc, (2 hdc, 17 dc, 2 hdc) in next ch-9 sp, sk next sc, sc in next sc, sk next sc; rep from * 3 more times, omitting final sc from last rep, sl st in first sc to join.

Rnd 4: Ch 1, sp-sc (see Stitch Guide) over first sc, *ch 5, sk (2 hdc, 3 dc), sc in next dc, picot (see Stitch Guide), [ch 5, sk 4 dc, sc in next dc, picot] 2 times, ch 5, sk (3 dc, 2 hdc), sp-sc over next sc; rep from * 3 more times skipping sp-sc at end of last rep, sl st in first sp-sc to join.

Fasten off and weave in loose ends. Block as needed.

SIX-POINT MEDALLION

Ch 2, 12 sc in 2nd ch from hook, sl st in first sc to join—12 sc.

Rnd 1: Ch 3 (count as dc), sk first sc, dc in next sc, ch 3, [dc in next 2 sc, ch 3] 5 times, sl st in top of beg ch-3 to join.

Rnd 2: Sl st in next dc and ch-3 sp, ch 3 (count as dc), ([yo, insert hook in next st and pull up lp, yo and draw through 2 lps] 2 times, yo, draw yarn through all 3 lps on hook [bobble made at beg of rnd], ch 3, bobble [see Stitch Guide]) in same ch-3 sp, ch 7, *(bobble, ch 3, bobble) in next ch-3 sp, ch 7; rep from * 4 more times, sl st in top of first bobble to join.

Rnd 3: Work 2 sl st in first ch-3 sp, ch 1, sc in same sp, *(6 dc, picot [see Stitch Guide], 6 dc) in next ch-7 sp, sc in next ch-3 sp; rep from * 5 more times skipping sc at end of last rep, sl st in first sc to join.

Fasten off and weave in loose ends. Block as needed.

FINISHED SIZE Six-point medallion—5¼" (13.5 cm) diameter. Moorish medallion—4¼" (11 cm) square.

YARN Worsted weight (Medium #4), about 15 yd (14 m) for each.

Shown here: Cascade 220 Wool (100% wool; 220 yd [201 m]/100 g): # 2413 (red) and # 2433, less than 1 skein each.

HOOK Size E/4 (3.5 mm). Adjust hook size as needed to obtain the correct gauge.

NOTIONS Tapestry needle.

GAUGE See finished sizes.

STITCH GUIDE

Spike single crochet (sp-sc): Insert hook 2 rnds below st indicated (i.e., into top of st from first rnd, yo, pull lp through and up to height of current rnd, yo, draw through both lps on hook.

Picot: 3ch, sl st into 3rd ch from hook.

Bobble: [Yo, insert hook in st and pull up a loop, yo and draw through 2 lps] 3 times in same st, yo, draw yarn through all 4 lps on hook.

sorbet
SCARF

*J*uxtaposing a vintage shell edging with contemporary, bright colors results in a cheerful, luscious three-season accessory. Wear it open as a dazzling wrap or bunched up around the neck as a cozy, whimsical scarf.

FINISHED SIZE 67" (170 cm) long and 12½" (32 cm) wide.

YARN Sportweight (Fine #2): About 547 (500 m) main color and 301 yd (275 m) trim color.

Shown here: Sheep Shop Sheep 3 (30% silk, 70% wool, 325 yd [297 m]/3.5 oz): sherbert G123 (multi; A), 2 hanks, and Boy F69 (blue; B), 1 hank.

HOOK Size G/6 (4.25 mm). Adjust hook size if necessary to obtain the correct gauge.

NOTIONS Tapestry needle.

GAUGE 2 (shell and ch-5 sp) and 14 rows = 4½" (11.5 cm) in shell patt after blocking.

stitch guide

+ SHELL (SH)
5 dc in next st.

SCARF

With A, ch 48.

Row 1: (RS) Sc in 8th ch from hook, sc in next 2 ch, *ch 5, sk 3 ch, sc in next 3 ch; rep from * to last 2 ch, ch 2, dc in last ch, turn—21 sc.

Row 2: Ch 1, sc in first dc, *ch 3, sk next sc, sc in next sc, ch 3, sc in next ch-5 sp; rep from * across, working last sc in 5th ch of tch, turn.

Row 3: Ch 1, sc in first sc, *sc in next ch-3 sp, ch 5, sk next sc, sc in next ch-3 sp, sc in next sc, sc in next ch-3 sp, sh (see Stitch Guide) in next sc, sc in next ch-3 sp, sc in next sc; rep from * to last 2 sc, sc in next ch-3 sp, ch 5, sk next sc, sc in next ch-3 sp, sc in next sc, turn.

Row 4: Ch 1, sc in first sc, *ch 3, sc in next ch-5 sp, ch 3, sk next sc, sc in next sc, ch 3, sk next sc, sk next 2 dc, sc in next dc, ch 3, sk next 2 dc, sk next sc, sc in next sc, rep from * to last ch-5 sp, ch 3, sc in next ch-5 sp, ch 3, sk next sc, sc in next sc, turn.

Row 5: Ch 5, sc in first ch-3 sp, sc in next sc, sc in next ch-3 sp, *ch 5, sk next sc, sc in next ch-3 sp, sc in next sc, sc in next ch-3 sp, rep from * to last sc, ch 2, dc in sc, turn.

Row 6: Ch 1, sc in first dc, *ch 3, sk next sc, sc in next sc, ch 3, sc in next ch-5 sp; rep from * across, working last sc in 3rd ch of tch, turn.

Row 7: Ch 1, *sc in next sc, sc in next ch-3 sp, sh in next sc, sc in next ch-3 sp, sc in next sc, sc in next ch-3 sp, ch 5, sk next sc, sc in next ch-3 sp, rep from * to last 3 sc, sc in next sc, sc in next ch-3 sp, sh in next sc, sc in next ch-3 sp, sc in next sc, turn.

Row 8: Ch 1, sc in first sc, *ch 3, sk next sc, sk 2 dc, sc in next dc, ch 3, sk 2 dc, sk next sc, sc in next sc, ch 3, sk next sc, sc in next ch-5 sp, ch 3, sk next sc, sc in next sc, rep from * to last sh, ch 3, sk next sc, sk 2 dc, sc in next dc, ch 3, sk 2 dc, sk next sc, sc in next sc, turn.

Row 9: Rep Row 5.

Rep Rows 2–9 twenty-four more times. Rep Rows 2–8 once more.

Last row: Ch 3, sc in first ch-3 sp, sc in next sc, sc in next ch-3 sp, *ch 3, sk next sc, sc in next ch-3 sp, sc in next sc, sc in next ch-3 sp, rep from * to last sc, ch 1, hdc in last sc, turn.

Fasten off and weave in loose ends.

EDGING

Join B with sl st in last ch of foundation ch.

Rnd 1: Work 43 sc evenly spaced across foundation, 3 sc in tch, turn work 90 degrees, work 315 sc evenly spaced up long edge of scarf, 3 sc in tch of last row, turn work 90 degrees, work 43 sc evenly spaced across short end of scarf, 3 sc in last st of last row, turn work 90 degrees, work 315 sc evenly spaced down long edge of scarf, 3 sc at end of side, sl st in first sc to join, turn—728 sc.

Rnd 2: Ch 1, sc in first sc, 3 sc in next sc, *sc in each sc to next 3-sc corner group, 3 sc in middle sc; rep from * around, sc in each sc to end, sl st in first sc to join, turn—736 sc.

Rnd 3: Sl st in next sc, ch 1, sc in next sc, *ch 5, sk next 3 sc, sc in next sc; rep from * to middle sc of 3-sc corner group, (sc, ch 5, sc) in middle sc, cont from * around, ch 2, dc in first sc to join, turn.

Rnd 4: Ch 1, sc in first dc, 9 dc in corner ch-5 sp, *[sc in next ch-5 sp, ch 5] 2 times, sc in next ch-5 sp, 7 dc in next ch-5 sp; rep from * to 3 ch-5 sps before corner, [sc in next ch-5 sp, ch 5] 2 times, sc in next ch-5 sp, 9 dc in corner ch-5 sp, [sc in next ch-5 sp, ch 5] 2 times, sc in next ch-5 sp, 7 dc in next ch-5 sp, [sc in next ch-5 sp, ch 5] 3 times, sc in next ch-5 sp, 7 dc in next ch-5 sp, [sc in next ch-5 sp, ch 5] 2 times, sc in next ch-5 sp, 9 dc in corner ch-5 sp, *[sc in next ch-5 sp, ch 5] 2 times, sc in next ch-5 sp, 7 dc in next ch-5 sp, rep from * to 3 ch-5 sps before corner, [sc in next ch-5 sp, ch 5]

2 times, sc in next ch-5 sp, 9 dc in corner ch-5 sp, [sc in next ch-5 sp, ch 5] 2 times, sc in next ch-5 sp, 7 dc in next ch-5 sp, [sc in next ch-5 sp, ch 5] 3 times, sc in next ch-5 sp, 7 dc in next ch-5 sp, sc in next ch-5 sp, ch 5, sc in next ch-5 sp, ch 2, dc in first sc to join, turn.

Rnd 5: Ch 1, sc in first dc, ch 5, sc in next ch-5 sp, (dc, ch 1) in each dc of group to last dc, dc in last dc of group, [sc in next ch-5 sp, ch 5] 2 times, sc in next ch-5 sp, *(dc, ch 1) in each dc of group to last dc, dc in last dc of group, sc in next ch-5 sp, ch 5, sc in next ch-5 sp, rep from * to opposite side at center 3 ch-5 sps, ch 5, sc in

next ch-5 sp, cont from * around, end with (dc, ch 1) in each dc of group to last dc, dc in last dc of group, sl st in first sc to join, turn.

Rnd 6: *(2 sc, ch 2) in each ch-1 sp to last ch-1 sp, 2 sc in last ch-1 sp, ([sc, ch 2] 4 times, sc) in next ch-5 sp, rep from * around working ([sc, ch 2] 4 times, sc) in additional ch-5 sp at short ends, sl st in first sc to join. Fasten off and weave in loose ends.

FINISHING
Block scarf to desired measurements.

Edging

BAG
First Section
With A, ch 33.

Row 1: Sc in 2nd ch from hook and in each ch across, turn—32 sc.

Row 2: Ch 1, sc in each st across, turn.

Rows 3–32: Rep Row 2.

Begin shaping
Row 1: Ch 1, sc in first st, sc2tog (see Glossary), sc to end, turn—31 sc rem.

Row 2: Ch 1, sc to last 3 sts, sc2tog, sc in last st, turn—30 sc rem.

Rep Rows 1–2 until 1 st rem. Fasten off, leaving a long tail for sewing.

Second Section
Row 1: With B, work 32 sc along longest side of first section

placing 1 sc in each row-end of first 32 rows, turn—32 sc. Cont as for first section.

Third Section
With C, work as for second section.

Fourth Section
With D, work as for second section.

Assembly
With long tail at point of section threaded on a tapestry needle, sew sections tog as foll: With tail of A and using a woven seam (see Glossary), sew from point on section A to beg row of section B, leaving dec edges unattached. Rep for rem sections, using tail of B to attach it to section C, using tail of D to attach it to section D, and using tail of D to attach it to section A (see below).

DRAWSTRING
With D, ch 50, drop D and draw up lp of C for next ch, ch 50, drop C and join B, ch 50, drop B and join A, ch 50, turn. *With A, sl st in each ch of A, fasten off A; rep from * using B, then C, then D—200 sts.

UPPER BAG
With D, work 132 sc evenly around open top edge of bag, working 33 sc across dec edge of each color section—132 sc. Cont in sc in the rnd without joining rnds, working a total of 6 rounds each in D, A, and B. Join C and work 2 rnds in sc. Place marker (pm) in last st to mark end of rnd. Move m up as work progresses.

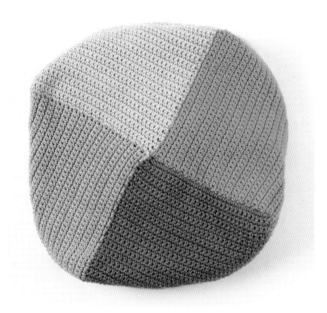

Next rnd: (drawstring eyelets) Sc in next 4 sts, *ch 2, sk 2 sc, sc in next 9 sts; rep from *, ending with sc in last 5 sts—12 ch-2 sps.

Next rnd: Sc in each sc, 2 sc in each ch-2 sp around—132 sc. Work 2 rnds even in sc. Fasten off.

FINISHING

Weave in loose ends. Weave drawstring cord through eyelets and then knot each end of cord with an overhand knot.

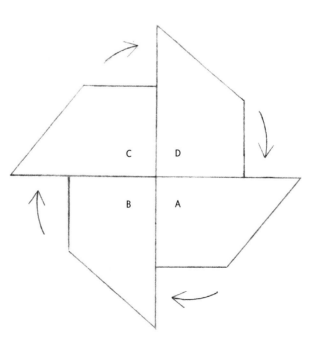

all-star
BLANKET

*C*heerful stars tumble across a cozy kid-size blanket. The squares are assembled as you crochet the last round of each motif, so there's no sewing at the end. A sophisticated palette of gender-neutral colors is combined with two simple versions of the motif arranged checkerboard style. For your young all-star, superstar, or rock star, make the perfect personalized gift by using his or her favorite colors or school or team colors.

FINISHED SIZE 37" (94 cm) wide and 49" (124.5 cm) long.

YARN Worsted weight (Medium #4), about 1,700 yd (1,555 m).

Shown here: NaturallyCaron.com Country (75% microdenier acrylic, 25% merino wool, 185 yd [170 m]/3 oz): silver service #0008 (A), 2 skeins; plum pudding #0022 (B) and spruce #0013 (C), 1 skein each; and naturally #0007 (D) and deep taupe #0015 (E), 3 skeins each.

HOOK Size I/9 (5.5 mm). Adjust hook size if necessary to obtain the correct gauge.

NOTIONS Tapestry needle.

GAUGE Star Motif through Round 5 (before edging and assembly) = 5" (12.5 cm) square.

Star Motif (finished, assembled, and blocked) = 6" (15 cm) square.

NOTE
✦ To keep this project portable for as long as possible, first crochet all the motifs through Rnd 5, then finish and assemble with Rnds 6–7.

+ **TREBLE CLUSTER (TR-CL)**— Yo twice, insert hook in back lp only (blo) of last st of star point and *pull up lp, [yo and draw through 2 lps on hook] 2 times* (2 lps on hook), sk sl st between star points, yo twice, insert hook in spare lp of first ch of next star point, rep from * to * (3 lps on hook), yo and draw through all lps on hook.

STAR MOTIF

Note: All rnds are worked with RS facing except Rnd 6. With A, ch 5, sl st in first ch to form ring.

Rnd 1: (RS) Ch 3 (counts as dc), 14 dc in ring, sl st in top of beg ch-3 to join—15 dc.

Rnd 2: Cont with A, [ch 5, sc in 2nd ch from hook, hdc in next ch, dc in next ch, tr in next ch, sk next 2 dc, sl st in next dc] 5 times, except end with sl st in sl st at beg of rnd, fasten off A—5 star points.

Rnd 3: Join either B or C in the tip of any star point as foll: insert hook in skipped ch at tip of star point under 2 strands of the sc row edge, sl st, ch 1, sc in same place, [working down the point, hdc through back lp only (blo) in next st, dc blo in next st, edc (see Glossary) blo in next st, tr-cl (see Stitch Guide), edc in next spare lp, dc in next spare lp, hdc in next spare lp, sc in skipped ch at tip of star point] 5 times except omit last sc, end with sl st in first sc to join, fasten off—40 sts.

Note: For randomly tumbling stars, occasionally vary the beg place of the next rnd from motif to motif.

Rnd 4: (RS) Join D with sl st in any st, ch 4 (counts as tr), [edc in next st, dc in next st, hdc in next st, sc in each of next 3 sts, hdc in next st, dc in next st, edc in next st, (tr, ch 2, tr) in next st for corner] 4 times except omit last tr, end with sl st in top of beg ch-4 to complete corner—4 corners.

Rnd 5: Cont with D, ch 1, sc in same ch as join, sc in each of next 10 sts, [(sc, ch 2, sc) in next ch-2 sp for corner, sc in each of next 11 sts] 3 times, (sc, ch 2, sc) in last ch-2 sp, sl st in first sc to join, fasten off D.

Make 47 more Star Motifs through Rnd 5 in the foll color scheme: 24 with Rnd 3 in B, 24 with Rnd 3 in C. Weave in loose ends before assembling.

Join Motifs

Note: In Rnds 6–7, try to keep your tension very relaxed, particularly the chains and joins, as this stitch tends to pull in.

Arrange motifs in a 6 × 8 square array, distributing the two color versions checkerboard style. Finish and assemble each motif across a row in turn, as foll:

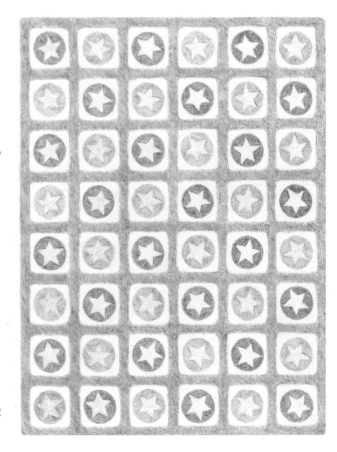

Motif 1

Rnd 6: (WS) Join E with sl st in any ch-2 corner sp, ch 1, sc in same sp, *ch 1, sc in next sc, [ch 1, sk next sc, sc in next sc] 6 times, ch 1, (sc, ch 2, sc) in next corner ch-2 sp; rep from * 3 times except omit last (sc, ch 2, sc) in corner, instead end with sc in same sp as beg, ch-1, sc in first sc to join, turn.

Rnd 7: (RS) Cont with E, ch 1, sc in sp made by last sc, *[ch 1, sc in next ch-1 sp] 8 times to next corner ch-2 sp, ch 1, (sc, ch 2, sc) in corner sp; rep from * 3 times except omit last corner and end with sc in same sp as beg, ch 2, sl st in beg sc, fasten off.

Motifs 2–48

After first motif is completed, all subsequent motifs are joined to each other during Rnd 7 at the 9 ch-1 sps along each side and at the corner ch-2 sps as foll:

Work Rnd 6 as for Motif 1.

Joining one side: Work Rnd 7 to first corner join, (sc, ch 1, sl st in corner sp of previous motif, ch 1, sc) in corner sp of working motif, *ch 1, sl st in corresponding ch-1 sp of previous motif to join, sc in next ch-1 sp of working motif; rep from * across to next corner sp, ch 1, sl st in ch-1 sp of previous motif, (sc, ch 1, sl st in corner sp of previous motif, ch 1, sc) in corner sp of working motif.

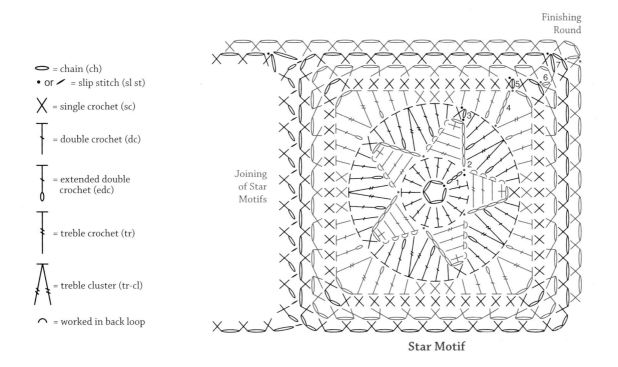

⬭ = chain (ch)

• or ╱ = slip stitch (sl st)

╳ = single crochet (sc)

╪ = double crochet (dc)

= extended double crochet (edc)

= treble crochet (tr)

= treble cluster (tr-cl)

⌒ = worked in back loop

Finishing Round

Joining of Star Motifs

Star Motif

Joining two sides: Work Rnd 7 to first corner join, [(sc, ch 1, sl st in corner sp of previous motif, ch 1, sc) in corner sp of working motif, *ch 1, sl st in corresponding ch-1 sp of previous motif to join, sc in next ch-1 sp of working motif; rep from * to next corner sp, ch 1, sl st in ch-1 sp of previous motif] 2 times, (sc, ch 1, sl st in corner sp of previous motif, ch 1, sc) in corner sp of working motif.

FINISHING

With WS facing, join E in ch-2 sp at any corner of blanket, ch 1, sc in same sp, *[ch 1, sc in next ch-1 sp] 9 times, ch 1, sc in corner ch-2 sp of same motif, ch 1, sc in corner ch-2 sp of next motif; rep from * around entire edge of blanket, making a corner of (sc, ch 2, sc) in each corner of blanket, end with sc in same ch-2 sp as beg, ch 2, sl st in beg sc, fasten off and weave in loose ends.

FAST FRIENDS BRACELETS

These little bracelets are great fun to make in all the colors of the rainbow. Inspired by the knotted friendship bracelets that were a mainstay of childhood summers, these quick versions can be classic or dainty, depending on whether you choose to work the optional third round.

BRACELET

Ch 72.

Row 1: Working in bottom ridge lp of ch, sl st in 12th ch from hook, *ch 5, sk next 5 ch, sl st in bottom ridge lp of next ch; rep from * across—10 ch-sps.

Rnd 2: Turn work 180 degrees and work in unused lps of foundation ch, sl st in next ch, ch 1, sc in same ch, sc in next 4 ch, sl st in next ch, *sc in next 5 ch, sl st in next ch or sl st; rep from * around both sides of Row 1, sl st in first sl st, ch 6 for buttonhole, sl st in same sl st to join.

Rnd 3: (optional) Sl st in next 3 sc, *ch 3, picot (see Stitch Guide), ch 3, sc in next (2 sc, sl st, 2 sc), sl st in next sc*; rep from * to * ending with sl st in last ch of first long side, sl st in next 5 sts, rep from * to * around, sl st in sl st at base of buttonhole to join.

Fasten off and weave in loose ends.

FINISHING

Wet bracelet and pin to desired shape. Sew button to end opposite buttonhole.

FINISHED SIZE About 7¼" (18.5 cm) wrist circumference and 1" (2.5 cm) wide.

THREAD About 15 yd (14 m) size 10 crochet thread. *Shown here:* Aunt Lydia's Classic Crochet Thread size 10 (100% mercerized cotton; 350 yd [320 m]/2 oz): aqua#450 or wasabi #397, 1 ball each.

HOOK Size 1 (2.75 mm) steel hook. Adjust hook size if necessary to obtain the correct gauge.

NOTIONS One ¼" (6 mm) button with shank, sewing needle, matching sewing thread.

GAUGE 39 sc = 4" (10 cm) in patt.

NOTES

+ To inc or dec length of bracelet, inc or dec beg ch by a multiple of 6.

Choose whether to fasten off bracelet after Rnd 2 for a simpler chain loop bracelet or complete Rnd 3 for a wider bracelet.

STITCH GUIDE Picot—Ch 3, sl st in 3rd ch from hook.

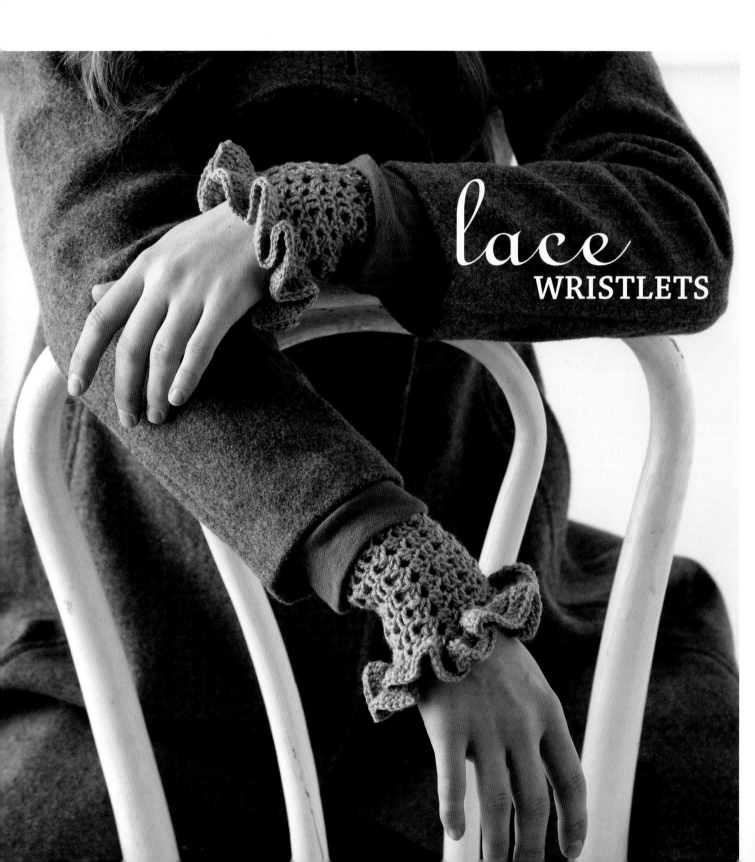

lace
WRISTLETS

$\mathcal{F}$ormal or flirty—or both—these feminine wristlets are the perfect gift for girls and women of all ages. Anyone who can do a double crochet can complete this pair in just a day or two, so they're the perfect last-minute gift. They look great under sleeves or over gloves all year round.

FINISHED SIZE 4¾" (12 cm) long from cuff to ruffle; 7½" (19 cm) circumference at cuff.

MATERIALS Sportweight (Fine #2), about 125 yd (114 m).

Shown here: Louet Gems Sport Weight (100% merino wool; 225 yd [206 m]/100 g): Neptune, 1 skein.

HOOK Size G/6 (4 mm). Adjust hook size if necessary to obtain the correct gauge.

NOTIONS Tapestry needle.

GAUGE 6 sts and 3 rows = 1" (2.5 cm) in dc.

+ SHELL (SH)
(2 dc, ch 2, 2 dc) in same space.

WRISTLET

Ch 43, leaving a long tail.

Rnd 1: Dc in 4th ch from hook, dc in each ch across, sl st in first dc to form ring, being careful not to twist sts—40 dc.

Rnd 2: Ch 3 (counts as first dc here and throughout), dc in first dc, ch 2, 2 dc in next dc, sk 2 dc, dc in next 2 dc, *sk 2 dc, 2 dc in next dc, ch 2, 2 dc in next dc, sk 2 dc, dc in next 2 dc; rep from * 3 times, sl st in 3rd ch of beg ch-3 to join—5 ch-2 sps.

Rnds 3–11: Sl st in first 2 dc and in first ch-2 sp, ch 3, (dc, ch 2, 2 dc) in same sp, *sk 2 dc, dc in next 2 dc, sk 2 dc, sh (see Stitch Guide) in next ch-2 sp; rep from * 3 times, dc in last 2 dc, sl st in 3rd ch of beg ch-3 to join, do not fasten off—5 sh.

Ruffle

Rnd 1: Ch 3, 2 dc in first dc, 3 dc in each dc and ch around, sl st in first dc to join—120 dc.

Rnd 2: Ch 3, 2 dc in next dc, *dc in next dc, 2 dc in next dc; rep from * around, sl st in first dc to join—180 dc. Fasten off and weave in loose ends.

babymoon
ROBE

$\mathcal{N}$ew mothers are showered with adorable gifts for their newborns, but they could use some care and attention themselves. This cozy knee-length robe is crocheted from the top down in three pieces to the underarms, then worked in one piece to the end. The cotton yarn is soft, cuddly, and easy to care for. Frog closures adorn the robe, and ribbon ties on the inside keep the front panels in place during wear.

FINISHED SIZE Sizes S (M, L, XL): 43 (47, 55, 59)" (109 [119.5, 139.5, 150] cm) bust circumference; to fit bust size 34–36 (38–40, 42–46, 48–50)" (81.5 [96.5, 112,127] cm).

YARN DK weight (Light #3), about 2,250 (2,550, 3,300, 3,600) yd [2,055 (2,329, 3,014, 3,288) m] cotton.

Shown here: Blue Sky Alpacas Skinny Dyed Cotton (100% organically grown cotton, 150 yd [137 m]/65 g): maize #307, 15 (17, 22, 24) skeins.

Note: Robe shown measures 36" (91.5 cm) long; additional yarn will be needed to work a longer robe.

HOOK Size F/5 (3.75mm). Adjust hook size if necessary to obtain the correct gauge.

NOTIONS Tapestry needle, 2" (5 cm) black frog clasp, two 20" (51 cm) lengths of ⅜" (1 cm) black ribbon, sewing needle, black sewing thread.

GAUGE 4 repeats and 8 rows = 4" (10 cm) in crosshatch patt (see Stitch Guide).

Note: Gauge is measured flat, not while hanging. Robe may grow in length when worn.

NOTE
+ Robe is worked from the shoulders down. Start by crocheting the upper right, upper left, and upper back pieces separately. Next, join the three pieces and finish the remainder of the body in one piece.

chain to upper left front, sc in first ch of next ch-3, ch 3, cont in crosshatch patt across left front to end, sc in tch, ch 10, turn—43 (47, 55, 59) ch-3 sps.

Row 3: 2 dc in 4th ch from hook, sk 3 ch, sc in next ch, ch 3, dc in next 2 ch, dc in next sc, cont as for crosshatch patt Row 2 to end, turn—44 (48, 56, 60) ch-3 sps.

Rows 4–5: Work even in crosshatch patt, turn.

Row 6: Work even in crosshatch patt, ch 10, turn.

Row 7: 2 dc in 4th ch from hook, sk 3 ch, sc in next ch, ch 3, dc in next 2 ch, dc in sc, cont as for crosshatch patt Row 2 to end, turn—45 (49, 57, 61) ch-3 sps.

Row 8: Rep Row 6.

Row 9–15: Rep Rows 3–8, then rep Row 3 once more—47 (51, 59, 63) ch-3 sps.

Work even in crosshatch patt to desired length. (See chart below for suggested length by height.)

Robe Length

Height	Rows from Neckline to Knee
5' (152.4 cm)	68
5'4" (162.6 cm)	72
5'7" (170 cm)	75
5'9" (175.3 cm)	78
5'11" (180.3 cm)	80

Shown in size 36" (91.5 cm) with 75 rows from neckline to knee; longer lengths may require additional yarn.

Fasten off and weave in loose ends.

Seam shoulders as foll: Line up upper-back and upper-right-front pieces together at the shoulders with RS tog, join yarn to neck edge of shoulder. Working through both layers at the same time, sl st across shoulder to the armscye. Fasten off and rep for 2nd shoulder. Turn right side out to beg sleeve.

SLEEVES

Row 1: (RS) With RS facing, join yarn at armhole edge of either shoulder seam, ch 3, 2 dc in same st, work 20 (22, 25, 28) crosshatch setup sts (see Stitch Guide) evenly around armhole, ending with sl st in bottom st of tch at the beg of the row, turn—20 (22, 25, 28) crosshatch sts.

Row 2: Ch 3, 2 dc in same st, work even in crosshatch patt ending with sc in bottom st of tch, turn.

Row 3–10: Rep Row 2.

Row 11: Work first 10 (11, 12, 14) crosshatch sts in est patt, then dec as foll: sk 3 dc, sc in first ch of next ch-3, ch 3, dc2tog (see Glossary) over next 2 ch, sk next sc, hdc2tog (see Glossary) over next 2 dc, sk next dc, hdc2tog over next 2 ch, sk (ch, 3 dc), sc in next ch, cont in est patt to end, turn—19 (21, 24, 27) crosshatch sts.

Row 12–18: Rep Row 2.

Row 19: Work first 9 (10, 11, 13) crosshatch sts in est patt, then dec as foll: sk 3 dc, sc in first ch of next ch-3, ch 3, dc2tog over next 2 ch, sk next sc, hdc2tog over next 2 dc, sk next dc, hdc2tog over next 2 ch, sk (ch, 3 dc), sc in next ch, cont in est patt to end, turn—18 (20, 23, 26) crosshatch sts.

Row 20–26: Rep Row 2.

Row 27: Work first 8 (9, 10, 12) crosshatch sts in est patt, then dec as foll: sk 3 dc, sc in first ch of next ch-3, ch 3, dc2tog over next 2 ch, sk next sc, hdc2tog over next 2 dc, sk next dc, hdc2tog over next 2 ch, sk (ch, 3 dc), sc in next ch, cont in est patt to end, turn—17 (19, 22, 25) crosshatch sts.

Row 28–34: Rep Row 2. Fasten off.

Rep for 2nd shoulder and sleeve.

FINISHING

With RS facing, join yarn at top corner of upper right front and work across neckline as foll: *sk 3 dc, 6 dc in next sc, sk 2 ch, sc in next ch; rep from * across upper right front to shoulder seam between upper right front and back, 3 dc in shoulder seam, rep from * across back of neck to shoulder seam between upper left front and back, 3 tr in shoulder seam. Work across upper left front, making tr shells in the "valleys" (the inc points) as foll: *sc at edge of the "hill" (the top of the tch where the row was inc'd at the end), then in valleys consisting of 2 rows, work 6 tr in the center of the valley; in valleys consisting of 4 rows, work 8 tr in the center of the valley. Rep from * across upper left front to the end of the increases, ending with sc in the top corner of upper left front.

Weave in loose ends. Block robe and allow to dry.

Lay robe flat and closed. Leaving the frog clasp closed, pin loop side of frog 1–2" (2.5–5 cm) below the upper right corner and the knot side of the frog to the upper left corner. To allow for a little extra ease in the bust if desired, pin the knot side closer to the edge of the inner flap. When the frog is pinned to the robe, unclasp and sew to the robe with sewing needle and thread.

Lay robe flat, with both sides open. Pin 1 length of ribbon to the inside right 10" (25.5 cm) directly below bottom of armhole. Pin the other ribbon to the inside left 10" (25.5 cm) down from armhole but only 1" (2.5 cm) in from the vertical edge. Sew both ribbons to the robe with sewing needle and thread. (These ribbons can be tied when the robe is worn so that the inner flap stays in place.)

COLOR CHAIN SCARF

This simple scarf is made up of chains that are connected with single crochet every three stitches to give it an interesting structure and excellent drape. The scarf shown here begins with a chain of 300 stitches and is 8 chains wide, but you can make it any length or width you want. Try different yarns and color combinations for a totally different look.

SCARF

With A, ch 300. Fasten off.

Row 1: With B, ch 10, sc in 10th st of A chain, *ch 3, sk 3 sts, sc in next st; rep from * to last 10 sts of A chain, ch 10, fasten off.

Row 2: With C, ch 14, sc in 13th st of B chain, *ch 3, sk 3 sts, sc in next st; rep from * to last 14 sts of B chain, ch 14, fasten off.

Row 3: With A, rep Row 1.

Row 4: With B, rep Row 2.

Row 5: With C, rep Row 1.

Row 6: With A, rep Row 2.

Row 7: With B, rep Row 1.

FINISHING

Weave ends into chain "fringe," pulling snug to cause the fringe to curl. Block as desired.

FINISHED SIZE About 2" (5 cm) wide and 46" (117 cm) long, including fringe.

YARN DK weight (Light #3), about 60 yd (55 m).

Shown here: Classic Elite Wool Bam Boo (50% wool, 50% bamboo; 118 yd [108 m]/50 g): #1603 flint (gray; A), #1672 artichoke green (B), and #1689 watermelon (C), 1 ball each will make several scarves.

HOOK Size F/5 (3.75 mm).

NOTIONS Tapestry needle.

GAUGE About 12 chain stitches = 2" (5 cm). Exact gauge is not crucial.

sisal spiral RUG

*T*his rug takes a classic crochet motif that might normally be found in doilies and delicate projects and gives it a twist with a bulky, nontraditional yarn. Sisal twine is a natural, durable fiber that is perfect for a rug that can be used indoors or out. When crocheting with sisal twine you'll notice that the fiber is stiff and crunchy; a thorough wet block at the end will magically transform your project from warped and crunchy to soft and flat. A unique housewarming gift!

FINISHED SIZE 36" (91.5 cm) diameter.

YARN Chunky (Super Bulky #6) cotton or jute, about 667 yd (610 m).

Shown here: Lehigh 1-ply 100% sisal bundling twine (2,250 ft [686 m] per spool).

HOOK Size N/13 (9 mm) aluminum hook. Adjust hook size if necessary to obtain the correct gauge.

NOTIONS Removable stitch markers (m); pins (for blocking); tapestry needle.

GAUGE 9 sts and 10 rows = 4" (10 cm) in sc.

First 5 rnds of patt = 7" (18 cm) diameter.

NOTES

+ Sisal is a stiff fiber that requires you to use a sturdy aluminum hook because plastic or wood hooks may break. If the fibers scratch uncomfortably at your fingers, wrap a strip of felt around your finger and secure it all the way around with tape.

+ The pattern is worked in a spiral with the RS facing unless indicated otherwise. Do not join at the end of the round. Place a marker (pm) as indicated and move the marker up as your work progresses.

+ Stitches in the second round are worked into the space between stitches rather than into the stitch itself. The lace rounds are worked into the stitch as usual.

RUG

Loop the yarn tail around the working yarn to form an adjustable ring; work all sts from Rnd 1 into the center of the ring.

Rnd 1: Work 12 dc in ring, place marker (pm) in last st to mark end of rnd (see Notes), pull tail to tighten ring—12 dc.

Rnd 2: 2 dc in each sp between (bet) stitches (see Notes), move m up—24 dc.

Rnd 3: *Sc in next 3 sts, ch 3, sk next st; rep from * around, skipping the last marked st, move m to last ch-3 sp—3 sc bet ch sps.

Rnd 4: *Sk next sc, sc in next 2 sc, 2 sc in next ch sp, ch 4; rep from * around—4 sc bet ch sps.

Rnd 5: *Sk next sc, sc in each sc to next ch sp, 2 sc in ch sp, ch 5; rep from * around—5 sc bet ch sps.

Rnd 6: *Sk next sc, sc in each sc to next ch sp, 2 sc in ch sp, ch 6; rep from * around—6 sc bet ch sps.

Rnd 7: *Sk next sc, sc in each sc to next ch sp, 2 sc in ch sp, ch 7; rep from * around—7 sc bet ch sps.

Rnd 8: Rep Rnd 7—8 sc bet ch sps.

Rnd 9: *Sk next sc, sc in each sc to next ch sp, 2 sc in ch sp, ch 8; rep from * around—9 sc bet ch sps.

Rnd 10: Rep Rnd 9—10 sc bet ch sps.

Rnd 11: *Sk next sc, sc in each sc to next ch sp, 2 sc in ch sp, ch 9; rep from * around—11 sc bet ch sps.

Rnd 12: Rep Rnd 11—12 sc bet ch sps.

Rnd 13: *Sk next sc, sc in each sc to next ch sp, 2 sc in ch sp, ch 10; rep from * around—13 sc bet ch sps.

Rnd 14: Rep Rnd 13—14 sc bet ch sps.

Rnd 15: *Sk next sc, sc in each sc to next ch sp, 2 sc in ch sp, ch 11; rep from * around—15 sc bet ch sps.

Rnd 16: Rep Rnd 15—16 sc bet ch sps.

Rnd 17: *Sk next sc, sc in each sc to next ch sp, 2 sc in ch sp, ch 12; rep from * around—17 sc bet ch sps.

Rnd 18: Rep Rnd 17—18 sc bet ch sps.

Rnd 19: *Sk next sc, sc in each sc to next ch sp, 2 sc in ch sp, ch 13; rep from * around—19 sc bet ch sps.

Rnd 20: Rep Rnd 19—20 sc bet ch sps.

Rnd 21: *Sk next sc, sc in each sc to next ch sp, 2 sc in ch sp, ch 14; rep from * around—21 sc bet ch sps.

Rnd 22: Rep Rnd 21—22 sc bet ch sps.

Rnd 23: *Sk next sc, sc in each sc to next ch sp, 2 sc in ch sp, ch 15; rep from * around—23 sc bet ch sps.

Rnd 24: *Sk next sc, sc in each sc to next ch sp, 17 sc in ch-sp; rep from * around.

Rnd 25: Sc around, working 2 sc in st at each tip, turn.

Rnd 26: With WS facing, sl st in each st around, sl st in first st to join. Fasten off and weave in loose ends.

FINISHING

Wet block (see Glossary) rug in the bathtub. Place the rug flat on a large towel and roll it up to squeeze out excess water. With WS facing, place rug on a dry towel, stretch each pinwheel panel and shape the tips until they lay flat, then pin to towel. Allow to dry. For a neat finish, trim wispy strands of fiber with scissors.

◯ = chain (ch)

• = slip stitch (sl st)

✗ = single crochet (sc)

┬ = double crochet (dc)

◯ = adjustable ring

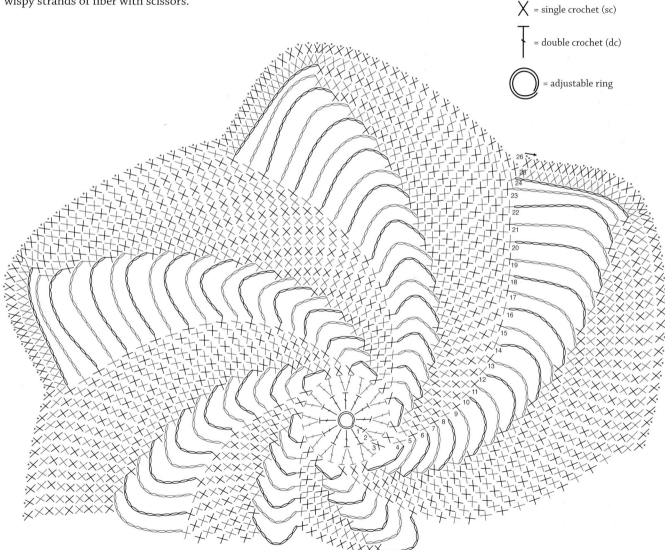

Reduced sample of Spiral Motif

glossary

CHAIN (CH)

Place a slipknot on hook. Yarn over and draw it through loop of slipknot. Repeat, drawing yarn through the last loop formed.

SINGLE CROCHET (SC)

Insert hook into a stitch, yarn over and pull up a loop (**Figure 1**), yarn over and draw it through both loops on hook (**Figure 2**).

Figure 1   Figure 2

SINGLE CROCHET 2 TOGETHER (SC2TOG)

Insert hook into next stitch, yarn over, pull up a loop (2 loops on hook); insert hook into next stitch, yarn over, pull up a loop (3 loops on hook). Yarn over and draw yarn through all 3 loops on hook (**Figure 1**). Completed sc2tog—1 stitch decreased (**Figure 2**).

Figure 1   Figure 2

SINGLE CROCHET 3 TOGETHER (SC3TOG)

[Insert hook into next stitch, yarn over and pull up a loop] 3 times (4 loops on hook), yarn over and draw through all loops on hook—2 stitches decreased.

EXTENDED SINGLE CROCHET (ESC)

Insert hook in next st, yarn over, pull up a loop (2 loops on hook), yarn over and draw through first loop on hook, yarn over and draw through both loops on hook.

REVERSE SINGLE CROCHET (RSC)

Beginning at the left edge, insert hook into next stitch, yarn over, pull up a loop (**Figure 1**), yarn over and draw through both loops on hook (**Figure 2**). Continue working from left to right (**Figure 3**).

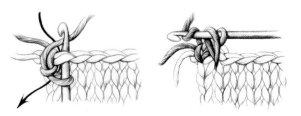

Figure 1   Figure 2

Figure 3

HALF DOUBLE CROCHET (HDC)

Yarn over, insert hook into a stitch, yarn over and pull up a loop (3 loops on hook), yarn over (**Figure 1**) and draw it through all the loops on the hook (**Figure 2**).

Figure 1   Figure 2

HALF DOUBLE CROCHET 2 TOGETHER (HDC2TOG)

[Yarn over, insert hook into next stitch, yarn over and pull up a loop] 2 times (5 loops on hook), yarn over and draw through all loops on hook—1 stitch decreased.

HALF DOUBLE CROCHET 3 TOGETHER (HDC3TOG)

Yarn over, insert hook into next stitch, yarn over and pull up a loop, [yarn over, insert hook into next stitch, yarn over and pull up a loop] twice (7 loops on hook), yarn over and draw through all loops on hook—2 stitches decreased.

DOUBLE CROCHET (DC)

Yarn over, insert hook into next stitch, yarn over and pull up a loop (3 loops on hook; **Figure 1**), yarn over and draw it through 2 loops (**Figure 2**), yarn over and draw it through the remaining 2 loops (**Figure 3**).

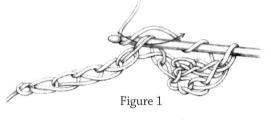

Figure 1

Figure 2

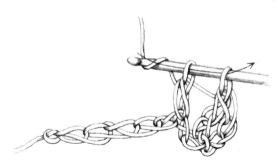

Figure 3

DOUBLE CROCHET 2 TOGETHER (DC2TOG)

Yarn over, insert hook into next stitch, yarn over and pull up a loop **(Figure 1)**, yarn over and draw yarn through 2 loops, yarn over, insert hook into next stitch and pull up a loop (4 loops on hook), yarn over, draw yarn through 2 loops **(Figure 2)**, yarn over and draw yarn through the remaining 3 loops on hook **(Figure 3)**—1 stitch decreased **(Figure 4)** or one cluster with 2 sts together.

EXTENDED DOUBLE CROCHET (EDC)

Yarn over, insert hook in next stitch, yarn over and pull up a loop (3 loops on hook), yarn over and draw through 1 loop on hook (3 loops on hook), yarn over and draw through 2 loops on hook, yarn over and draw through remaining 2 loops on hook.

TREBLE CROCHET (TR)

Yarn over 2 times, insert hook into stitch, yarn over and pull up a loop (4 loops on hook; **Figure 1**), yarn over and draw it through 2 loops **(Figure 2)**, yarn over and draw it through the next 2 loops **(Figure 3)**, yarn over and draw it through the remaining 2 loops.

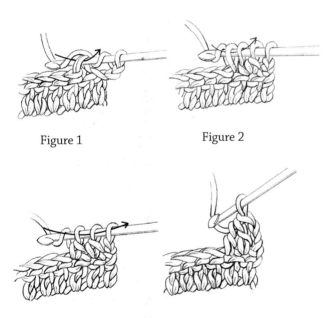

Figure 1   Figure 2

Figure 3   Figure 4

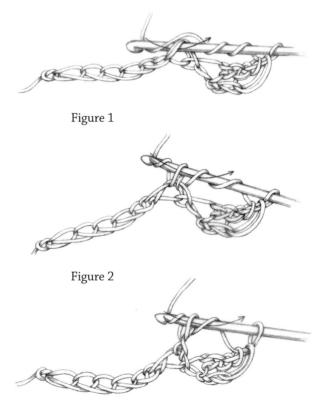

Figure 1

Figure 2

Figure 3

SLIP STITCH (SL ST)

Insert hook into stitch, yarn over and draw loop through stitch and loop on hook.

WHIPSTITCH

With right side of work facing and working through edge stitch, bring threaded needle out from back to front along edge of piece.

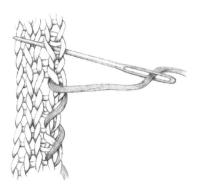

BACKSTITCH SEAM

Working from right to left, under edge stitch, bring threaded needle up through both pieces of fabric (**Figure 1**), then back down through both layers a short distance (about a row) to the right of the starting point (**Figure 2**). *Bring needle up through both layers a row-length to the left of backstitch just made (**Figure 3**), then back down to the right, in the same hole used before (**Figure 4**). Repeat from *, working backward one row for every two rows worked forward.

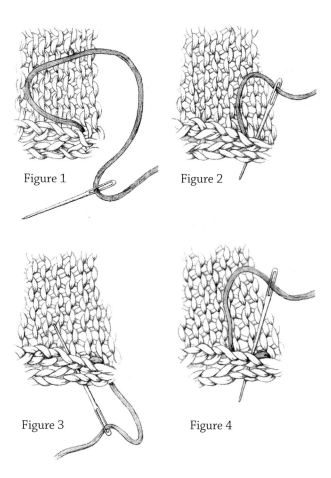

Figure 1

Figure 2

Figure 3

Figure 4

WOVEN SEAM

Place pieces side by side on a flat surface, right sides facing you and the edges lined up row by row or stitch by stitch.

Step 1: Secure seaming yarn on wrong side of piece A at start of seam. Pass needle to right side at bottom of first stitch.

Step 2: Put needle through bottom of first stitch of piece B and pass it up to right side again at top of stitch (or in stitch above, if you're working in single crochet).

Step 3: Put needle through bottom of first stitch of piece A, exactly where you previously passed needle to right side, and bring needle to right side at top of same stitch.

Step 4: Put needle through piece B where you previously passed needle to right side, and bring needle to right side at the top of same or next stitch.

Step 5: Put the needle through piece A, where you previously passed needle to right side, and bring needle through to right side at top of stitch.

Repeat Steps 4 and 5, gently tightening seam as you go, being careful not to distort fabric. Allow rows to line up but don't make seam tighter than edges themselves. Edges will roll to the wrong side of work. Secure end of seaming yarn.

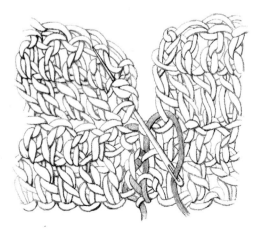

ZIPPER

With RS facing and zipper closed, pin zipper to fronts so front edges cover the zipper teeth. With contrasting thread and RS facing, baste zipper in place close to teeth **(Figure 1)**. Turn work over and with matching sewing thread and needle, stitch outer edges of zipper to WS of fronts **(Figure 2)**, being careful to follow a single column of sts in the knitting to keep zipper straight. Turn work back to RS facing, and with matching sewing thread, sew knitted fabric close to teeth **(Figure 3)**. Remove basting.

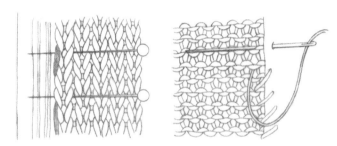

Figure 1   Figure 2

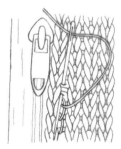

Figure 3

contributing designers

ERICA ALEXANDER learned to crochet from her home ec teacher longer ago than she likes to admit. She stills enjoys finding places to use single crochet in interesting ways.

An engineer by trade, **ROBYN CHACHULA** uses her building processes to design crochet projects in Cincinnati, Ohio. Check out her books *Blueprint Crochet: Modern Designs for the Visual Crocheter* (Interweave, 2008) and *Mission Falls Goes Crochet* (2008) for more of her architecturally inspired designs.

DORIS CHAN'S sons loved stars, so she made up the star motif featured in this book years before becoming a crochet designer. She has since wandered into garment design for magazines, yarn companies, and two books, *Amazing Crochet Lace* and *Everyday Crochet* (Potter Craft 2006 and 2007).

KAREN DROUIN has been crocheting and knitting for more than thirty years and has taught classes in both needle-crafts. She is a member of the HHCC (a Crochet Guild of America chapter in Connecticut) and is working to become a professional member of CGOA. Making items for the American Angels group and for a local church and hospital keeps her busy in her spare time.

Striving for more balance in her life, **MEGAN GRANHOLM** is a crochet designer by night and an accountant by day. Yarn and hook are always in her pannier as she bicycles around Corvallis, Oregon. Visit her blog at loopdedoo.blogspot.com.

JENNIFER HAGAN'S first craft was crochet, thanks to her Granny Kate. Having tackled many other crafts through the years, she now only makes time for crochet and knitting. Visit Jennifer's design line, Figheadh Yarnworks (figheadh .com), which she runs from her Pacific Northwest home with her husband, Fred. *Figheadh sona dhut agus crochet sona dhut!* (Happy Knitting and Happy Crocheting!)

KATIE HIMMELBERG crochets and knits in Loveland, Colorado, while her son naps.

JULIE ARMSTRONG HOLETZ is a crochet designer and the author of two books, *Uncommon Crochet: Twenty Five Projects Made from Natural Yarns and Alternative Fibers* (Ten Speed Press, 2008) and *Crochet Away!* (Price Stern Sloan, 2006). She plays and crochets in the Seattle area with her husband and two children. Find out what Julie is up to on her blog at skamama.com.

DONNA HULKA has been creating things with her own two hands since she was a little girl. Originally from Maryland, she now lives in North Carolina with her husband, young son, and dog. You can say hello to Donna and see more of her handiwork at her website, yarntomato.com.

KATHRYN MERRICK has sold yarn at the Tomato Factory Yarn Company and Simply Knit. She has cut fabric for Liza Prior Lucy's online company Glorious Color. She now designs for magazines and books and is writing her own book, *Crochet in Color* (Interweave, 2009). She lives in the Philly 'burbs, surrounded by much yarn and lots of music.

ANNIE MODESITT lives and works in St. Paul, Minnesota, with her family and assorted pets. Her first craft love was crochet, to which she loves to return whenever possible! Annie blogs about her life as a designer at anniemodesitt.com.

LISA NASKRENT is the designer of the Crochet Garden at crochetgarden.com. Take a stroll through the garden and watch your hook come alive.

CHLOE NIGHTINGALE lives in Scotland and collects kitschy retro crochet paraphernalia. Visit her website at galvanic .co.uk and add her as a friend on Ravelry.com.

KRISTIN OMDAHL is the author of *Wrapped in Crochet: Scarves, Wraps & Shawls* (Interweave, 2008). Her designs have been featured in many other books and magazines. See her innovative knit and crochet pattern collection at StyledByKristin.com.

CHRISTINA MARIE POTTER has a bachelor's degree in fashion from Stephens College. She designs both knit and crochet patterns and teaches classes. She resides in St. Louis with her husband and daughters. You can see her work online at christinamariepotter.com.

TONI REXROAT loves creating handmade gifts for friends and family. The simple, elegant lines of the bracelet she designed for this book guarantee she will be gifting many to close friends.

KIM WERKER writes and crafts in Vancouver, Canada. Founder of CrochetMe.com, former editor of *Interweave Crochet,* and co-host of *Knitting Daily TV,* she enjoys staring at the big picture and imagining all the amazing possibilities. This is her sixth crochet book. Keep up with her creative adventure at kimwerker.com.

SANDI WISEHEART loves to play with crafts of all kinds. She and her husband are on a mission to fill their lives with friends, fiber, yarn, beads, animals, and laughter in Toronto, Canada.

MYRA WOOD is an internationally known teacher, fiber and bead artist, designer and author. She was a regular guest on *Knitty Gritty* and *Uncommon Threads.* Her work has been published in a wide range of books and magazines including her own book, *Creative Crochet Lace* (Woodworks Editions, 2008). Find galleries of her work at myrawood.com.

JILL WRIGHT learned to knit and crochet at an early age, loving each craft equally. She later discovered felting and began further experimentation. She enjoys freelance knit and crochet design and is always exploring new stitch variations, constantly fascinated by the fact that such beautiful items can be made by manipulating yarn and hook. You can visit Jill's website at woolcrafting.com.

sources for yarn

Artistic Wire Ltd.
752 North Larch Ave.
Elmhurst, IL 60126
(630) 530-7567
artisticwire.com
Craft wire

Aunt Lydia's
Distributed in the United
States by Coats and Clark
8 Shelter Dr.
Greer, SC 29650
coatsandclark.com
*Aunt Lydia's Fashion Crochet
Thread*

Blue Sky Alpacas
PO Box 88
Cedar, MN 55011
blueskyalpacas.com
*Skinny Dyed Cotton
Sport Weight*

Brown Sheep
100662 County Rd. 16
Mitchell, NE 69357
brownsheep.com
Lamb's Pride

Cascade Yarns
PO Box 58168
1224 Andover Pk. E.
Tukwila, WA 98188
cascadeyarns.com
Cascade 220

Classic Elite Yarns
122 Western Ave.
Lowell, MA 01851
(978) 453-2837
classiceliteyarns.com
Wool Bam Boo

DiVé
Distributed in the United
States by Cascade Yarns
Autunno

Handmaiden Fine Yarn
handmaiden.ca
Sea Silk

Jade Sapphire
jadesapphire.com
Lacey Lamb

Karabella Yarns Inc.
1201 Broadway
New York, NY 10001
(800) 550-0898
karabellayarns.com
Lace Merino Silk

Lanaknits Designs
Hemp for Knitting
320 Vernon St., Ste. 3B
Nelson, BC V1L 4E4
Canada
Allhemp6 Lux

Lehigh
Lowe's Stores
lowes.com
Lehigh Sisal Binder Twine

Lorna's Laces
4229 N. Honore St.
Chicago, IL 60613
lornaslaces.net
Shepherd Sock

Louet North America
3425 Hands Rd.
Prescott, ON
Canada K0E 1T0
louet.com
Gems Sport Weight

Malabrigo Yarn
malabrigoyarn.com
Worsted

NaturallyCaron.com
naturallycaron.com
Country

Patons
320 Livingstone Ave. S.
Listowel, ON N4W 3H3
Canada
(888) 368-8401
patonsyarns.com
SWS

Red Heart
Coats & Clark
8 Shelter Dr.
Greer, SC 29650
redheart.com
Eco-Ways

Rowan Yarns
Distributed in the United
States by Westminster
Fibers
165 Ledge St.
Nashua, NH 03060
westminsterfibers.com
Cotton Glace
Pure Wool DK

Sheep Shop Yarn Company
PO Box 1444
East Greenwich, RI 02818
sheepshopyarn.com
Sheep Shop 3

ShibuiKnits
1101 SW Alder St.
Portland, OR 97205
shibuiknits.com
Sock

index